P9-DXO-515

RICH CHURCH POOR CHURCH

KEYS TO EFFECTIVE FINANCIAL MINISTRY

J. CLIF CHRISTOPHER

Abingdon Press
Nashville

RICH CHURCH, POOR CHURCH
KEYS TO EFFECTIVE FINANCIAL MINISTRY

Copyright © 2012 by Abingdon Press

All rights reserved.

No part of this work may be reproduced or transmitted in any form or by any means, electronic or mechanical, including photocopying and recording, or by any information storage or retrieval system, except as may be expressly permitted by the 1976 Copyright Act or in writing from the publisher. Requests for permission can be addressed to Permissions, The United Methodist Publishing House, P.O. Box 801, 201 Eighth Avenue South, Nashville, TN 37202-0801, or emailed to permissions@umpublishing.org.

Library of Congress Cataloging-in-Publication Data has been requested.

ISBN 978-1-4267-4336-8

Scripture quotations unless otherwise noted are from the Common English Bible. Copyright © 2011 by the Common English Bible. All rights reserved. Used by permission. (www.Com monEnglishBible.com)

Scripture quotations noted NRSV are from the New Revised Standard Version of the Bible, copyright 1989, Division of Christian Education of the National Council of the Churches of Christ in the United States of America. Used by permission. All rights reserved.

12 13 14 15 16 17 18 19 20 21—10 9 8 7 6 5 4 3 2 1

MANUFACTURED IN THE UNITED STATES OF AMERICA

This book, and indeed my whole life, is dedicated to Aaron, Drew, Rebekah, and Tricia. You four children have chosen lives that make me incredibly proud. Your love of Christ, the church, your families, and your chosen work make me a very rich man indeed. You are my most precious treasure.

CONTENTS

INTRODUCTION

A pastor friend of mine commented the other day that if he were ever truly successful he might find himself out of work. I asked him what he meant, and he said, "Well, I preach for persons to be faithful followers of Jesus Christ. If they all started doing that, then I would be out of work." My reply back was that if and when he found himself unemployed, we would both celebrate.

I find myself writing another book around the topic of Christian financial stewardship because I have been unsuccessful with my past efforts. Indeed, if all those who call themselves Christians and members of a church would start tithing tomorrow, I would be out of work. My company might cease to exist, or our mission focus might become a whole lot more fun and rewarding. Instead of helping churches acquire funds, we would be in the business of helping them be faithful in their distribution. We would spend a lot more time assisting them in formulating a plan to spend most efficiently what they have in their storehouses. We would discuss how to feed the hungry, clothe the naked, house the homeless, care for the sick, and restore the prisoner. We would be a community of believers fully devoted to Jesus Christ as our Lord and Savior, overjoyed at the opportunity to be his servants to the world around us. What fun that would be.

But alas, we are not there. My company is not about to go out of business, and few of the pastors I know will not be needed once again to preach this Sunday. This book was written because we do not give as Christ taught us to give, and that is because Jesus is not yet the Lord of our lives. The church finds itself in serious trouble financially, not so much because of a lack of money, but because of a lack of passion and commitment to One other than ourselves.

The statistics are screaming to us that we are in great jeopardy if significant change does not take place:

- Religion used to receive 60 percent of all charitable gifts in America. Today it receives 32 percent.

- Charitable giving as a whole is down from $315 billion in 2007 to $298 billion in 2011.[1]

- United Methodists give an average of 1 percent of their income to the church. Presbyterians give the same percentage. Episcopalians and Lutherans give 1.1 percent. Baptists are all the way up to 2 percent. Those of the Orthodox and Catholic faiths give less than 1 percent.[2]

- In a study done in 2008, it was found that baby boomers give about 15 percent less than their parents gave at the same age (using current dollars). The lack of giving is most pronounced with religion.[3]

- Giving to congregational finances is down 22 percent since 1968, and giving to benevolences in the same time period is down nearly 50 percent.[4]

- Financially healthy churches totaled 31 percent of all churches in 2000, but only 14 percent of churches by 2010, which is a drop of over 50 percent.[5]

I could go on and on with statistics that point out that the American church is in serious financial trouble and without serious change could move into irrelevancy. It appears that I will have a job for a while longer.

Rich Church, Poor Church describes the characteristics I see in most of our churches, which are always behind financially and searching for money (Poor Church), compared to what I witness in churches that are not always struggling to find resources for mission and ministry (Rich Church). It could just as easily have been called *Healthy Church, Sick Church* or *Vital Church, Insignificant Church*.

This book is not written by a researcher. I have never had the patience to do good research. It is written by an observer. Over the last forty years, as a pastor for twenty years and now as the president of Horizons Stewardship Company, I have been afforded an opportunity to work with thousands of churches, pastors, and laypersons. I have begun to see common traits among those churches with resources and also among those that never seem to have resources. You are free to disagree with me, and I am sure many will. I have only my own eyes and ears to back up my findings.

My highest hope for this book is to get you, as a church leader, to ask questions. Questions about the condition of your church and its vitality need to be asked. Explore whether your church is on the rich or poor side of the scale and why. If you need to make changes, then how can those changes best be done? At a minimum, I simply hope that after reading this book, you will not remain as you are. As far as the church goes, this has not worked out so well lately. What we are called to be and do is far too important not to do it well.

The initial chapter reviews my previous writings regarding why people give. I still find far too many church leaders who are working on the answer to the question, "Why should I give?" and not on the right question for today, which is, "Why should I give to you?" If we can't learn how to answer that question, then our Poor Church will never become a Rich Church.

The chapters following deal with areas that separate the haves from the have-nots. I will cover how the Rich Church focuses on mission rather than survival, compelling communication rather than facts communication, debt principal rather than debt payments, asking rather than not asking, humility rather than arrogance, high expectations rather than low expectations, knowing the facts on our donors rather than just guessing on the donors, being transformational in talk rather than obligatory, and pastors taking the lead. At the end of each chapter is a series of discussion questions that will hopefully stimulate groups to wrestle with the condition of their church and to develop solutions.

Jesus has died and has been resurrected. The Holy Spirit has been sent to be among us. Martyrs by the thousands have died to bring us to where we are today. The church is the living body of Christ in the world, and we are a part of it.

Praise God from whom all blessings flow. There is no excuse to be poor anymore!

NOTES

1. Giving USA, *The Annual Report on Philanthropy* (Indianapolis: Indiana University, 2011).

2. Patrick M. Rooney, "Dispelling Common Beliefs about Giving to Religious Institutions in the United States," in *Religious Giving: For Love of God*, ed. David H. Smith (Bloomington: Indiana University Press, 2010).

3. Noted by Russell James in *Advancing Philanthropy* (April 2008).

4. *The State of Church Giving through 2008* (Champaign, IL: Empty Tomb, Inc., 2010).

5. David A Roozen, *A Decade of Change in American Congregations 2000–2010* (Hartford, CT: Hartford Institute for Religious Research, 2011).

CHAPTER ONE

WHY GIVE TO THE CHURCH?

I was working with a pastor of a midwestern Protestant church, assisting his recruiting persons to serve in an upcoming capital campaign. A few weeks before, he and I reviewed the candidates and determined those we thought would be the best fits for his campaign. The campaign was not an exciting one. The funds would primarily be used to do delayed maintenance on the facility and replace some old HVAC systems. The church's operating budget had no room to absorb these expenses, so the church was calling on a capital campaign to produce the revenue. I felt that we had a pretty good lineup of active laypersons who would do their best to lead in the campaign. Each one was asked to come in for a thirty-minute session with the pastor and me to hear what the job would entail and hopefully to say yes to serving.

The third person we met on the first morning of recruiting was someone who I felt would be a slam dunk to serve. She had been the immediate past chairperson of the board and a member of the church for the last twenty years. She and her husband were the third largest donors to the church. I did not anticipate any problem.

The pastor quickly introduced us and asked her to take a seat. He then asked to me to explain the job in a bit more detail. I did so in about five minutes while the church member listened politely, but with a serious look on her face. I expected to get a quick positive answer and to move on to the next candidate. It was not to be.

After I finished, she let silence enter the room, and then spoke: "Pastor, thank you for the confidence you have shown in me. I am honored to be asked to serve. As you know, my husband and I have been a part of this church for a long time, and we have always been happy to serve. We have obviously known of this upcoming campaign and have talked at length about what might be expected of us in it. I have some concerns.

"We have always supported the church financially and, we think, faithfully. Last year, however, we also began supporting World Vision and Oxfam. We have been very impressed with some of the work they are doing around the world and the difference it seems they are making. We are considering increasing that support. At the same time, we have been observing that our church seems to be getting smaller. I know that worship attendance is down this year from last year, and I think last year was down from the year before that. I can't remember when I last saw a youth or adult baptized at our altar. Just looking around on Sundays, it seems that we are getting older and older. I see a lot more persons with gray hair or no hair than children. Pastor, can you honestly tell me that my church is the best place for me to give?"

I was stunned but also very interested in how her pastor

2

would answer this probing question about the future of his church. I leaned back to watch the drama unfold.

The pastor squirmed in his seat a bit and began to stammer out some words about how grateful he was for them and how much he valued her willingness to share with him. I think he repeated that about four times. He talked about his appreciation for the two organizations she mentioned and said he agreed that they did good work. He stumbled on for another minute or two and then finally got to her question. His answer was, "I think Clif might help us answer that question." He turned to me and smiled.

I did not know what to do for a moment. I knew that she did not want to hear from me. She was well aware of who I was and that I was temporarily at her church. She knew I did not even live in her state. I could not embarrass the pastor, however, so I babbled a bit about the "body of Christ" and such, and when I quit talking, she thanked us both and said she would get back to the pastor in the morning with her answer.

After she left the office, he looked at me and asked, "Do you think she will serve?" "No, she will not," I answered. "However, she has done you a great favor. She has given you the question that you must be prepared to answer if you have any hope for success in this campaign." He nodded and then asked me if I had a template to assist him. I could only shake my head and wonder if I could make it to the end of the campaign.

This woman was a giver. She was a devoted member of the church and, as far as I could determine, a faithful follower of Jesus Christ. She felt, however, that she had a stewardship responsibility to use the gifts God had given to her and her husband in a wise way. She wanted her money to make a difference on behalf of the kingdom of God. She wanted a return on her investment. She wanted to feel that what she gave would change lives and transform the world into a better place. She asked the question that more and more church members are asking: "Is my church the best place for me to invest to make a difference and change lives?" Her pastor was not prepared to answer the question.

In far too many churches, pastors still preach that persons should just give to the church, without spelling out why. Every seven days people drop money into the plate and never really understand what difference it makes. Outside of the church, people hear and see compelling stories of healing, feeding, rescuing, saving, and helping. They are inundated with one solicitation after another from the charitable world and told heartwarming stories about how lives are being changed daily by the work of these agencies and organizations. People can understand and often personally relate to these stories.

Meanwhile the church continues to promote itself with word that the budget is up 3 percent, and we want all members to increase giving by 3 percent.

Often, our message does not inspire or convince. The message comes without faces or names. It emphasizes guilt and obligation. Scripture is quoted as a means of compelling a person to give. But nowhere is the case made as to why the Lord, who gave you all that you have, would want you to invest those gifts in this church.

Our donors are asking if the Lord was not at work in the hospital that served them with a new heart for Grandpa. Was the Lord not at work with the counselor at the college who helped keep their daughter from dropping out? Was the Lord not at work with the rescue mission that gave the homeless man a bed on the night when it was below freezing outside? Was the Lord not at work in the hospice foundation's caregiver who stayed tirelessly with Mother as she breathed her last breath? How is the Lord at work in my church? Just because it says "church" and has a cross does not mean the work of the Lord is being done there or only there. Why should I give to the church?

Nonprofits understand very well why persons give and what motivates continued giving. The church, by and large, seems afraid to compete. If the church does not learn to compete, however, it will find that fewer and fewer will be choosing them, and gifts will be moved to those who most effectively convinced them to contribute.

Why do persons give?

I have written extensively about this in *Not Your Parents' Offering Plate*. It is, however, important to restate this elementary understanding before one can fully understand the balance of this book, which will contrast the Rich Church and the Poor Church. The groundbreaking book *Born to Raise* by Jerold Panas featured research on the topic of why people give. Nonprofits have studied and been shaped by this research. Church leaders have predominantly ignored it to their detriment.

A BELIEF IN THE MISSION OF THE INSTITUTION

The number one reason that people give is a belief in the mission of the institution. People give when they can see a difference created that they value. If they have a heart for young people, they will give to the institution that they believe is most helping young people become the adults the donors believe are good for society. If they have a heart for the world's hungry, they will give where they believe the hungry are best being fed. If they have a heart for whales, they will give to the organization that convinces them they are the best at saving whales.

Nonprofits are well aware of this number one reason that people give, and they do their best at every turn to promote in understandable ways how they are accomplishing their mission. The youth organization will not send out a news-letter telling persons how many youth came by to play ball or how many members they now have. They will put on the cover of their newsletter a story of one youth whose life was turned around from participation in its program. People don't relate to program numbers. They relate to changed lives.

The hunger organization doesn't tell you data on how many persons they fed in so many countries and in so many days. They feature the face of one child and tell you how the child's mother brought him to the food center and how a worker intervened in his life with nourishment, to the point that he is now running and playing with other children. One can easily see how this life has been changed. The whale organization doesn't tell you what a new boat cost or what one trip to sea will mean in diesel fuel. They feature a picture of a giant blue whale leaping in the air and tell you how that whale was saved through action they took in the Pacific Ocean. In other words, they help convince you that they are doing the mission they advertise.

What is it that a church advertises when it puts a cross on the sign and the word *church* on the front door? What do persons understand the mission to be? Is the church telling compelling narratives about its mission and how they are doing that mission well? The pastor in the Midwestern church could not make the case. Can your church?

REGARD FOR STAFF LEADERSHIP

The second chief reason why people give is a regard for staff leadership. The number one rule in fundraising is that people give to people. They know that programs and buildings do not change lives, but people do. They must feel confident in the leadership to guide the institution in fulfilling the mission. Key investors in institutions want an intimate relationship with the CEO, and this is why nonprofits demand that their leader relate and connect with those able to help them fund their mission.

Many churches want to defy this reasoning, acting like persons of wealth should not desire a trusting relationship with their leaders (pastors). These Poor Churches pretend that lack of information about donors is a good thing for its leaders. They even set up policies that say that no pastor shall know what persons give, making it impossible for a pastor even to say a thank-you to a donor for a major gift, as if being thanked is not helpful or polite.

No college would encourage its president not to be aware of who its main alumni supporters are. No hospital would keep a CEO who does not set specific time aside for relating to those persons who have built new wings or who could establish new programs that would help the hospital do its mission.

In church after church I see pastors asking singers to join the choir, parents to help in the youth program, those who have recreational skills to coach teams, and people with mission hearts to lead mission teams, but I do not see them intentionally spending time with those who are blessed financially and asking them to share those blessings with the church. What is the difference? People want to hear why they should support the church. Many churches are not even in line.

FISCAL RESPONSIBILITY OF THE INSTITUTION

The third chief reason why people give is the fiscal responsibility of the institution. People do not want to give to an organization that wastes their money or always seems to be short of money. This sends a message that we are not able to do our mission, and achieving the mission is the number one reason why persons give. People do not want to give to a sinking ship but to one that might actually arrive at a destination.

This is why no nonprofit sends out messages that it is broke and in need of being saved from drowning. Donors do not want to just prop up an institution; they want to enable it to change lives. Nonprofits do not air their dirty laundry to the public. They deal with financial issues in private boardrooms and continue to talk publicly about how they are doing their mission.

Poor Churches, on the other hand, seem to believe that the more they cry wolf, the more they will get support. They publish financial data in their bulletins and newsletters that invariably show that the church is running a deficit. They say things such as, "50 percent of the year is complete, but we only have 40 percent of our revenue in." They always have about 40 percent in at the halfway mark because December is by far the largest giving month. They act as if they don't know that, believing that donors will give more if they think the church is broke. The exact opposite is true.

Pastors of these churches get up in the pulpit and tell people how bad it is or trot out the finance chairperson to do the same, somehow believing that this will make people want to throw their wallets at the altar. The exact opposite is true. This tactic encourages persons to avoid touching their wallets for fear of giving their money to a losing cause.

Amazingly, more church leaders are concerned at running a surplus than a deficit. Their fear is that if persons knew that the church actually had funds on hand they would stop giving. The fact is, if the church shares this good news, along with how it plans to use the gifts to change lives, people might give even more.

It is no wonder that many donors to the church are wondering if they should continue to give. They never hear stories of lives being changed like the ones they hear from other charities. Church leaders don't visit or ask for funds. Potential donors have little or no personal relationship with their pastor, unlike the one they have with the president of a college or the administrator of a hospital or the local director of Boy Scouts. They continue to get a message of gloom and doom that leads them to think that there is not much future in this place and perhaps their funds would be better invested elsewhere.

To have any hope at all of being a Rich Church, understand why people give.

QUESTIONS FOR YOUR CHURCH

1. How are you sharing stories about how you are changing lives?

2. Are your stories personal and shared in a way that is heartfelt and compelling to a donor?

3. Is the pastor as involved with persons of financial blessing as he or she is with persons with other gifts? Is there a reluctance to ask for financial gifts more than for talent gifts? Why?

4. Does your church subtly send a message that you are always in trouble financially? Is it possible that persons could perceive that the leadership is not a good manager of their funds? Do you publish deficit reports for all to see?

5. How would you answer a person who might ask you why he or she should give to your church?

CHAPTER TWO

KNOW THE MISSION

RICH CHURCH	POOR CHURCH
Mission	Survival
Lives	Money
Service	Facility
Discipleship	Appeasement
Jesus	Church

MISSION VS. SURVIVAL

The Rich Church, the healthy church, is always focused on its mission. Everything revolves around the mission. The mission keeps persons of varied backgrounds and with varied needs united. The mission is what causes things to get done and becomes the measure by which all things are judged.

The Poor Church, the sick church, is always focused on its own survival. Rather than describing the mission, their message to donors is what they require to survive. The primary goal is to balance the budget, regardless of how little is done. A balanced budget is the rule by which they determine their success and thus gain assurance of their survival.

In 1991, I had the opportunity to go to the Gulf War with the First Armored Division. I was in a MASH unit attached to combat support for the ground offensive in that conflict. On the day we landed in Saudi Arabia and every day we were there, I was reminded of the warrior ethos of the army:

I will always put the mission first

I will never accept defeat

I will never quit

I will never leave a fallen soldier on the field of battle

Every staff meeting that I attended centered on the mission: to remove the Iraqi army from the sovereign nation of Kuwait. Each time we gathered to review plans, it was that overall mission that guided how those plans were constructed. In staff meetings the supply officer reported on whether he had enough supplies to do the mission. The intelligence officer reported on whether he had enough information to do the mission. The sergeant major reported on whether he had the personnel to do the mission. I was asked to report on the morale and spiritual welfare of the troops to do the mission. The mission was always first.

If in one of those meetings someone brought up something that seemed outside the box, the commander would always interject, asking what that had to do with the mission. If it was not congruent to the mission, it was dismissed. I could have brought up that I would like to have air conditioning in my tent and that my cot was about four inches too short, but I would get nowhere because air conditioning and a more comfortable cot were not necessary for us to accomplish our mission. Taking care of me was also not our mission. Our mission was outside of us. It was them.

While serving in the army, I constantly reflected on how a mission focus was absolutely critical to success. The army believed that absolutely nothing was more important than mission first, and nothing was allowed to distract from that understanding. As a chaplain and one whose life has been spent in the church, I wish we had more of the attitude of the army in our churches. What if all our members had the attitude that joining this organization meant that they would always place mission first?

In the Rich Church, this is exactly what you see. There is a keen awareness that the customers are outside their walls and certainly not themselves. Every meeting focuses on how activities contribute to the mission. This mission is well known by everyone in the church. It is what unites, and it is what drives each decision.

A pastor in one of our Rich Churches told me the other day that a decision had been made in his church to change the style of worship in one of their four Sunday morning services. It meant that persons who were attending that service would either have to adapt to a different style or have to start attending church at a different hour than they were accustomed to. As one might imagine, this decision was neither made lightly nor received with delight by those who would have to change. They called for a meeting with the pastor and some of the decision-makers on a Sunday afternoon. The meeting began with various worship participants talking about how they would be affected and why they liked things the way they were. When they had calmed down, the pastor stood and reminded all those present of what their mission was. Their mission was to take Christ to those who did not know him. The entire rationale for changing the worship style was the evidence that they had a better chance of reaching these persons—or doing the mission—with a different style at that time. It focused the argument away from personal preference to "mission first." He told me that at first they grumbled, but once they realized that doing the mission had to come first and that could be the only point of discussion, the meeting ended and the church marched on, focused on the mission.

In the Poor Church, most of the thought and rhetoric around changing the worship service centers on what is best for the survival of the church as it now is. What will ensure that all those who are here now will stay here? What will ensure that no one will take their money and run? What will keep us from getting into financial trouble? The church focuses on how it can best keep things from changing because the church at least knows it is alive in the present. This is a church that is dedicated to keeping its soldiers happy and content. It is a church that will lose the battle and the war. This is a church that does not even realize they are in a war.

The mission of the church is fairly simple. Jesus gave it to us in Matthew 28. We are to go forth and make disciples of all persons and teach them to obey all that he taught us.

There is nothing complicated about this mission. It is a mission easily measured in lives. When the church makes a disciple, it has evidence because one goes from never claiming Christ as her or his Lord and Savior to making a profession of such. Her or his life then becomes one of living for the Master and Lord, Jesus Christ. Some churches call it a profession of faith, and others call it being born again. Whatever it is called, it is simply the changing of a person from following themselves as lord to following Christ as Lord.

I worked with a church that had been identified by its denomination as a Poor Church. The church was in serious financial trouble. The church members were significantly divided. They had gone through several pastors in a short period of time. Their worship attendance had declined for five straight years. They had a big building, but I could not see how it was being used for Kingdom work. My job was to try to diagnosis the problem and design solutions.

The pastor and four of his key leaders came in to the conference room where we were to meet. After a pleasantry or two, I offered them some of my observations from data they had submitted. One of those observations was that they had a budget of $1.6 million, and they had two persons accept Christ over the course of an entire year. I said, "You spend $800,000 per profession of faith. Do you feel you are getting good results from your spending priorities?" There was a pause in the room, and then the finance chairperson asked, "What is a profession of faith?" I sat silent to see if someone would answer his question. No one spoke up. I finally said, "It is when someone chooses Christ as their Savior for the first time." He looked at me, puzzled, and asked with seriousness, "Why would we count that?" I knew that I had diagnosed the problem.

This was a church that had no clue as to why it existed. When I talked to them about their church's strengths, they talked about fellowship and good friends. One man noted that they had the best chef in town. When I asked them about their weaknesses, they said they had been unable to balance the budget for the last two years and hoped I would help them trim and come up with ways for those who gave nothing to start giving. Mission to them was not the answer to their problems—it was money. What was their hope from their time with me? To learn some ways to survive.

LIVES VS. MONEY

Rich Churches are always talking about how they are changing lives. Poor Churches are always talking about how they need more money. Rich Churches understand that transforming lives, not raising money, is their business. Money is always seen as a tool for mission.

I attended worship at a Rich Church, and after singing some very spirited songs, everyone was asked to sit. Immediately on their video screen appeared a map of the world with a star on the spot where the church was located. Suddenly an arrow came out from the star and zoomed over to Africa. The picture then switched to a church member holding a small child. He began: "Hi, Church, it is Robbie, and I am in the Sudan working with Charlie here and others like him who have fled from the war. We are putting some weight on him and also putting a smile on his face. From me and Charlie. Thanks, Church."

The screen went back to the map, and another arrow traveled from the church over to New Jersey. "Hi, Church, this is Jackie. I am here in Newark with five of my church friends, and we are working in an inner-city mission, training persons on how to go on interviews and dress to get hired. What a thrill it was yesterday to hear from two of our patrons here who now are gainfully employed. We held a service last night to give thanks to God, and three persons have asked to be baptized this Sunday. God is good! Thanks, Church."

I watched as two more arrows flew out, showing where persons in the church were changing lives and serving Christ outside the walls of the church. It lasted about ninety seconds and left an indelible impression on me. Without even talking about money, I noticed that ushers were passing buckets around the worship center. I certainly wanted to contribute. I had just seen evidence that showed me this church was changing lives in powerful ways. I felt that my gift here would contribute to changing lives and making the world a better place.

Another Rich Church I visited for worship did not have as fancy a production on its video screen. But after their opening songs, the screen revealed a young man sitting in a chair, surrounded by a black drape. He simply began to talk about his prior life of addiction. He reflected on how lost he felt and even his two attempts at suicide. Then he told how his last friend in the world sent him a bus ticket to come home. When he arrived, his friend witnessed to him about the need for Christ to have control of his life. The friend got him to church and eventually to the moment when he gave his life to Jesus and got into Alcoholics Anonymous. Today that young man is the worship leader of the congregation. It was the first time most had ever heard his testimony. The pastor followed this witness by saying this was just one of many whom he as pastor was blessed to see on a regular basis at the church. He thanked the congregation for the support they give that changes lives. The church then took up the offering. I sure felt good about contributing to a church doing that kind of work.

Not long after, I worshiped in a Poor Church. After the songs were sung, the congregation was invited to sit. The finance chairman came forward to apprise the congregation of the current state of the church. He noted the size of the budget and what amount they needed to have collected by the present date. Next he shared what had actually been collected and the size of the deficit. He sounded a gentle alarm about at-risk programs, the possibility of releasing staff, and the fact that the denomination's fees had not been paid. He encouraged everyone to give more money if they possibly could and left the pulpit after reassuring everyone that the budget would be balanced and monies would not be borrowed to pay the bills. The pastor then came back to share the Scriptures and sermon. It was hard for me, however, to get over the facts shared by the finance chair and give much thought to anything else in the service. When the church called for the offering, we were again reminded of the need for more money. I was convinced that the mission of this church was not changing lives. It was getting more money. I was not very interested in this mission.

SERVICE VS. FACILITY

In the Rich Church, you hear a lot of emphasis placed on how it can be of service, and in the Poor Church, you hear a lot of emphasis on how it should be caring for its facility.

When churches call me for the first time, I usually ask the person calling to tell me about their church. You learn a lot from the first words uttered. What I hope to hear is how they understand themselves to be the living embodiment of Jesus Christ to the world around them. What service they feel they have been called to perform. What is the condition of the society around them that they feel they must minister to? I am hoping to hear language of sacrifice and heart for others. How do they see themselves carrying the cross? When I hear language like this, I know I have a Rich Church.

What I hear more often than I like is something like this: "We are the oldest congregation in the northwest corner of our state. We have been right here for over one hundred years. We have been referred to as the 'Cathedral of the Northwest.' Persons come to visit us to take pictures of the stained glass windows or the organ that was installed in 1889. Four governors have stood in our pulpit at one time or another, and a senator and two congressmen came out of our congregation. At one time we had one thousand people in worship every Sunday; but, of course, those days are gone."

This church is in love with its tradition and its facility

more than with Jesus, and exists today to care for a museum and to keep the memories alive. It is getting smaller every year because new persons do not care much for tradition, nor do they have fond memories of the erection of a facility over one hundred years old. The Daughters of the American Revolution or Sons of the Confederacy might find the place inviting, but others are not so much into history as they are looking for spiritual nurture and hope in today's world. This is a Poor Church destined to get poorer and poorer as the oldest pass on and no one is left to pick up the mantle.

DISCIPLESHIP VS. APPEASEMENT

In the Rich Church, there is an understanding that the customer is not currently within the walls of the church. The customer is someone who has never attended or has never accepted Jesus Christ as his or her Lord and Savior. In the Poor Church, you will hear of discipleship, but in reality the dominating decision-making factor is appeasement.

I was at an initial assessment of a church, sitting in the pastor's office. As we reviewed data that he had previously sent, I noted the church's mission statement: "We will make disciples of Jesus Christ for the transformation of the world." I said to him, "That is a very biblical mission statement." He seemed pleased at my compliment and went on to say that it was not very original but it had been adopted by the church at a leadership retreat the previous year. We continued to review what was going on in this church. The demographics showed that it was in a growing area that had numerous young families living within a couple of miles of the church.

A junior high school was located one block down and across the street. Visibility was good, and their facility was more than adequate to accommodate growth. I then asked him, "As the pastor, who do you feel is without Christ in your community that you need to minister to the most?" He quickly shot back, "Oh, we all know it is the young families. They are really struggling with raising their kids, paying the bills, keeping marriages together, and all those young-family issues." I then commented to him that the average age of his church was close to sixty and that it did not seem that many of those young families were a part of the church now nor were they about to join anytime soon. He agreed.

"Therefore," I said, "How do you see the church fulfilling its mission?"

"I want to start a more contemporary service, weekday child care, and an Upward basketball program." "Well," I said, "that sounds like some excellent ideas to excite and get you in front of that crowd. What is stopping you?" "The Simpsons and the Walkers,"[1] he said. "They are vehemently opposed to any sort of worship that is not traditional and does not use the hymnbook. The child care program might get through, but no basketball, because Rotary and one other group use our hall and it would require too much maintenance money to keep it clean." I looked a bit stunned, and he shook his head. "But what about the mission of making disciples?" I asked.

"That is the mission on paper because it looks good. The real mission of this church is to make sure that these two families are kept happy and that their money keeps flowing.

They make a big deal of paying all of our denominational dues each year. No one else wants to risk losing that money. There are certainly some folks who don't like this, but no one wants to be the one who takes responsibility or the nails on this one."

This church had me in because they were struggling to make ends meet. Because of two families, they managed to pay most of their budget each year, but the budget was meager for a church of that size. Persons outside the church could see what was going on and did not want any part of it. They wanted and needed a place to connect them with Almighty God, not two almighty families. Therefore, new funds did not come in from new families. The church would continue to get smaller and smaller and poorer and poorer, which is fine with the two families, because the fewer persons and the less money the church has, the easier it is to control. This church exists for a number of reasons, but Jesus is not one of them. They can sing "Stand Up, Stand Up For Jesus" on Sunday, but to really do so, they must first stand up stand up to the Simpsons and the Walkers.

To be a Rich Church you must be committed to the mission of making disciples, not appeasing persons.

JESUS VS. CHURCH

In the Rich Church, you hear a lot of talk about Jesus: "It is because of Jesus that we are beginning this ministry"; "It is because of Jesus that we feel called to do the following"; "It is because of Jesus that we have set up this program this way"; "It is because of Jesus that we are constructing this facility."

The talk is unashamedly about the One whom each one has pledged to follow.

In the Poor Church, the conversation is entirely different. The discussion is about what the "church" needs. We need to do this to keep the church alive. We need to get this going so that we will have a church on this block in ten years. We need to do this so our church will look nice on Sunday morning. We need to be mindful of the church's reputation. The motivation to act is for the preservation of the church. The question is, for what?

In my very first preaching class, I had a professor who taught the class that at the end of each sermon we should ask ourselves the question, "So what?" In other words, what do we want to happen in response to what we have just said? At the beginning and the end of meetings at the church, we should ask, "What purpose does this serve?" If we do this, how does it advance the cause of Jesus Christ? Is it Jesus who would have us make this change? Is it Jesus who is calling us to change? Is it Jesus who wants us to spend this money?

While still a very green preacher in my early twenties, I was sent to serve a church in a rural county seat. It was not a very big church, but to the members there it was the most important church in the world. I was excited to be their pastor.

I remember preaching my first sermon and hearing the nice words at the close of the service. I was on cloud nine. I returned that evening at the scheduled time for youth group only to find there were no youth. I asked around and was told that it had been several years since the church had had any kids attending on Sunday night. I was disappointed and wanted to change things. I went to the local junior high and high school and got acquainted with the youth. I hung out at ball practice and was a part of every game. Finally I decided to launch my plan and get some youth started in church. I got a grill, some hot dogs, a cooler full of soft drinks, and a neat video and sent out the call for kids to come. The first night about ten showed up. They got a few more kids to come, and they got a few more, and soon I had about twenty-five coming every Sunday night. I was excited. We kept having hot dogs or pizzas or sloppy joes, and this seemed to help attendance with growing kids with bottomless stomachs. A couple of months into this new venture I started to hear rumblings: "The church sure seems dirty on Monday mornings"; "The kitchen sink had mustard in it when we went to prepare for the ladies luncheon"; "Who is paying for all this food these kids are eating?" It was not very pleasant, but I just kept on.

About a month later it hit the fan. Worship had ended about two hours before, and I received a phone call at my home. When I answered, the lady on the other end of the line sternly said to me, "Brother Clif, a number of us at the church have been talking, and we all agree that we have a problem and you can solve it." "Yes, ma'am," I meekly said. "What is the problem?" She went on: "The church is not nearly as clean as it once was. We have to scrub down our kitchen at least once a week. We want a rule passed that says that no youth shall come to our church on Sunday evenings whose family is not a member of the church."

I was shocked and did not understand what would motivate such a request. "Why do you think we should do this?" I asked.

She replied about as quickly as I got my question out, "Because those of us who belong are having to pay for this food and we are having to pay for the church to be kept clean and the church needs to be there for us when we need it, not for persons who are not giving to keep it up."

Being extremely naive, I said to her, "Why don't we try to look at this like Jesus might look at it?" and she retorted just as soon as I said the name *Jesus,* "You leave him out of this!"

To her it had nothing to do with Jesus. It had everything to do with her church, and the two were simply not related. In the Rich Church, everything is about and for Jesus. That is what persons want to support. In the Poor Church, it is almost never about Jesus. Just the church!

QUESTIONS FOR YOUR CHURCH

1. Do all of your people understand what the mission of your church is?

2. Is this mission a unifying factor in your church?

3. How much discussion in your business meetings is about money, and how much is about changing lives?

4. Using a business meeting to create an honest assessment, name what business you are in.

5. Does your communications center around survival of the church or the mission of the church?

6. Are there persons or issues that control actions more than the need to make disciples?

7. From your personal perspective, do you think the leadership tends to talk more about doing for the church or doing as Jesus would command?

8. How can your church move toward being more focused on mission versus survival, money, facility, or pleasing certain factions?

NOTE

1. Not their real names.

CHAPTER THREE

WHO IS LEADING?

RICH CHURCH	POOR CHURCH
Compelling Communication	Facts Communication
God Led, God Talk	Numbers and Percentages
Vision of a New World	Vision till 5:00 P.M.

COMPELLING COMMUNICATION VS. FACTS COMMUNICATION

The Rich Church understands how to create compelling communication for its donors. The Poor Church bombards its people with facts that generally move no one. It boils down to an understanding of the sender and the message. The Rich Church understands whom it works for. The Poor Church seems to have different bosses and decision-making processes, depending upon the circumstances. People are a part of a church because they want to be a part of God's work and God's plan. They do not fully understand what that is or exactly where they may fit in, but they are in the church to find out and to be a part of something much bigger than themselves. Compelling communication in the church connects the decision or the need to the Almighty. When people understand that the call is from God and that they are being asked to be a part of his work, they will commit. When they only feel that they are being asked to get numbers to a certain place or to make something a bit more attractive, they simply contribute. The Rich Church is always looking for commitments. The Poor Church settles for contributions.

GOD LED, GOD TALK VS. NUMBERS AND PERCENTAGES

In the Rich Church, communication strategy begins with, "God is calling us to..." or "In my time of prayer and devotion I have felt that God wants more of us than he is getting and we should..." The pastor does not shy away from being the prophet/leader. The pastor does not hesitate to share that he or she feels that God is leading the church in a certain direction that requires a certain action. It does not mean that everyone will suddenly snap to and blindly follow, but it shows conviction, and it forces the hearers to debate the call of God, not a personal preference or certain facts.

In the Poor Church, communications begin with, "We have a problem and need to find a solution"; "Our entryway needs to have a nicer appearance and I thought we might..."; "That church that is growing so fast has a children's center that is state-of-the-art"; "We have 500 families and only 350 give anything. We need to get more to give."

What is compelling about that? Whose message is it? In

one church I heard, "We have not grown in ten years." What does this have to do with anything?

One evening during my college days a friend asked me if I would like to move down to his dorm room for the weekend because his roommate was going to be throwing a party off campus in a space he had rented. He would not be back until Sunday night. I thought that would be fun and told my friend to count me in. His roommate just happened to be the son of the governor of the state. As he was leaving to go host his party, he told us to pledge not to tell anyone, especially his parents, what he was going to do that weekend. Naturally, we pledged not to tell, like all good college friends do. Then we set off to create a neat weekend for ourselves.

About midnight we started getting prank phone calls for the "governor's son." They were seemingly from other college students playing a joke by threatening him with some sort of political revenge. At first, we brushed it off and then thought that we should call "the son" and tell him what was going on. We did, and he said he would notify security at the governor's mansion and not to worry about anything.

The calls kept coming about every ten minutes or so, until it reached 2:00 in the morning. We decided that on the next call, we would not just hang up but talk back. The phone rang. A voice on the other end said, "Where is Brent?" I quickly and curtly said, "I am not going to tell you!" Again the voice said, "You will tell me right now where he is!" I replied, "And just who do you think you are?" The voice calmly said, "I am the governor of the state of Arkansas, son. The national guard and all the state police work for me. Now where is he?" I told him.

It was very compelling when I understood who was sending the message.

Harrods department store in London is one of the largest department stores in the world. It occupies an entire block in downtown London with the exception of one corner that is occupied by a small chapel. There is a story that the board of directors of Harrods wanted to expand the store, and felt they needed to purchase the chapel in order to do this. A registered letter was sent to the chapel.

Dear Members of the Chapel:

The Board of Directors of Harrods has determined that it is in our best interest to expand next year. Your chapel currently occupies the site we want to use for our expansion. We are prepared to offer you fair market price for your little chapel and even throw in additional capital to assist you in relocation. We wish to move forthwith and seek your answer in the next two weeks.

Sincerely,

The Board of Directors of Harrods

Within a week a registered letter came back to Harrods from the little chapel. It read:

Dear Harrods:

We, the Board of Directors of the Little Chapel, are in receipt of your letter wishing to purchase our property. We have occupied this site for well over one hundred years. We have recently determined that it is in our best interest to expand next year. Your department store occupies the site we want to use for our expansion. We are prepared to offer you fair market price for your store and even throw in additional capital to assist you in relocation. We wish to move forthwith and seek your answer in the next two weeks.

Sincerely,

Cadbury

Cadbury Chocolate was at that time the largest chocolate manufacturing company in the world, and Mr. Cadbury was one of the richest men in the world. He happened to attend the little chapel. The directors at Harrods thought the letter was humorous until they saw who had sent it. Upon seeing that it was sent by someone who could back it up, it became far more compelling. It is important to know who is sending the message.

In the church, when it seems the message is coming only from the pastor or from one faction in the church, it is often ignored or given little consideration. When, however, it is clear that the message is coming from God, it demands attention. Far too many times we send out messages that are full of facts about a building or about money. What people want to know is whether it is about God or not. When they understand and believe that it *is* about God, it becomes compelling communication.

VISION OF A NEW WORLD
VS. VISION TILL 5:00 P.M.

The Rich Church constantly holds out a vision that is grand and bold about what God is doing and is going to do. There is talk about "Promised Land," "No more tears," and lions that lie down with lambs. They consistently invite persons to be a part of something much bigger than themselves. The communication is an encouragement for people to dream big and to work to fulfill those dreams of what the kingdom of God can be like.

The Poor Church seems to have no further vision than the end of the day. Their vision is to pay a bill or get through another Sunday. When you talk to these churches about what it is all about, they tend to stare at you with blank eyes. They have no conception of what God might want to do with them and frankly no belief that he would care to do anything with them. They are just a bunch of wanderers in the wilderness of church with no clear destination in mind. When the request goes out for people to fund the journey, it gets little response because no one knows where the journey is taking them.

The story of Joshua and Caleb (Numbers 13) is a good example of having a vision and understanding who sent it. Of the twelve spies who went to investigate the land that God had promised to deliver to the Israelites, only Joshua and Caleb saw the land from the view of the one who would deliver it. They saw the big picture and envisioned the new life in a new land. Because it was God who was calling them, they had every confidence that they would soon possess the land and prosper in it. The other ten just saw the short term. They saw the struggle against the current inhabitants and how hard the fight would be. Their confidence was only in themselves, and that was not much to go on. They were a majority, but they were wrong.

The Rich Church has a big dream because it believes in a big God. It is not afraid to be bold because it knows that it is not under its strength that victory is assured. The Lord leads it. The Rich Church is full of persons who are not controlled by a 401k or the economic conditions of the day. The Rich Church pays a lot more attention to prayer and the Bible than it does the *Wall Street Journal.*

QUESTIONS FOR YOUR CHURCH

1. When questions come up about the economy or other perceived obstacles to giving, does anyone remind persons of who is sending the message? Is the Bible referenced?

2. Who are the Joshuas and Calebs in your church?

3. When it comes to money matters, are your communications compelling from a faith point of view, or are they more about numbers and percentages?

CHAPTER FOUR

PRINCIPAL NOT PAYMENTS

RICH CHURCH	POOR CHURCH
Manage Debt Principal	Manage Debt Payments
See End	Only Sees the Year
Short Term	Long Term
Safety Net	No Net
"We" Will	"They" Will
Borrow 2X Raised	Build It... They Will Come

MANAGE DEBT PRINCIPAL VS. MANAGE DEBT PAYMENTS

I reviewed the financial report of a church with serious trouble meeting its budget and sustaining any kind of meaningful ministry. I noticed immediately that debt payments amounted to over 30 percent of the total budget. I asked the finance chairman to talk to me a bit about how this came to be.

"Well, it seemed like a good idea at the time," he began. "We had a dream of a new sanctuary along with a new family life center. It had been several years since we built any sort of facilities, and we felt that our building was a bit dated. When the architect showed us the design, it was dazzling. We all fell in love with it. At a town hall meeting the congregation just drooled over the plans. We ran a capital campaign and thought we did okay, but it was short of what had been targeted. As we discussed what to do, since we were about $2 million short of what we had read was ideal, it was mentioned that we could easily borrow all the money and not have to cut any of the project. No one wanted to cut anything since the people had been told they could have it all. It was then figured that we could make the payments from the campaign for the next three years and then with all our increased growth have another campaign in three years and start reducing the principal. It was scary, but we felt as though we were going to grow a lot, and we knew we could count on raising a lot of money since we had just had a pretty good campaign experience. It would take four to five campaigns, but we felt we could get it done. Everyone was so excited about a new sanctuary and a new family life center. We just knew they would keep giving. Now after six years we are not so sure."

As he spoke, I shook my head because I had heard this story before. "Please go on," I said.

"Well, several things happened. First, the cost of the building went about 15 percent over, which added $600,000 to the bottom line. Then our well-liked pastor of a dozen years left about the time the first campaign expired, and we had to launch the second one with a new pastor. She was all right, but she was just not like the one who had left. We began to lose people in attendance, and giving dropped. She is now gone, and we have our third pastor in six years. Then two years ago the appliance manufacturing plant closed, putting about 1,200 people out of work. Couple all of that with the economic downturn in the country, and we are struggling. We have cut half of our staff, which has really hurt the family life center because two of those staff members did programming in there. We have not paid anything on our denominational askings, and missions is darn near nonexistent. The new pastor is working hard but having a difficult time getting new persons in the door. So I guess that is why you are here. What should we do?"

My first reaction was to say that I wish they had asked six years earlier, because the hole they had now dug for themselves was going to be hard to get out of. I wish I could have stopped them before it got so deep. I felt a little bit like the oncologist who was looking at a lung cancer patient who had smoked for thirty years. Yes, there are some things we can do, but the real solution would have been for the patient to have made better decisions years ago.

Bad decisions regarding debt will cripple a church faster than just about anything. If you pick a bad pastor, it will hurt, but you can quickly move to get another one, which fixes that problem. A bad decision on a new ministry can be rectified after a few months, and with its elimination, the church can move on. But debt can be forever, and it is unforgiving. You just can't have a do over and have the same old church back once you have signed those papers.

The Rich Church understands that it needs to manage "debt principal." The Poor Church just looks at the "debt payments." It is always principal elimination that the church must have a plan for, not only making payments.

SEE END VS. ONLY SEES THE YEAR

The Rich Church always has a solid plan for exactly how it plans to pay off its debt. It sees how to get to the end. The Poor Church usually has no plan longer than making payments for a year and then hoping for the best. General Colin Powell was supposed to have counseled both Presidents Bush to never get into a war without knowing how you can get out. The same is true with debt. Never get into debt without a solid plan of how you can be out of debt *in seven years.*

SHORT TERM VS. LONG TERM

The Rich Church will never set itself up with long-term debt or with a long-term plan. It is very much aware that too many things can happen unexpectedly that can derail its ability to be the church and to perform ministry. It never plans on having debt for more than seven years, using two capital campaigns. The first campaign is to build the facility, and then the second is to pay off the debt. Planning on having more than two back-to-back capital campaigns is not a wise move.

The church referenced earlier became a Poor Church because it felt that every year going forward would be as good as or better than the current year. When rough times hit, everything changed except the debt, which stayed the same.

SAFETY NET VS. NO NET

The Rich Church enters into debt with a safety net. It does not stretch itself to the max. This way when things change going forward, the church has options and doesn't find itself in a corner with nowhere else to go. The Poor Church stretches itself to the maximum, owing so much for so long that multiple capital campaigns are the only way forward, even if external circumstances say that a campaign is not a good idea. The church finds itself so stretched that all things become subordinate to the debt. It cannot add staff for the facility, and sometimes it cannot even open the facility because it cannot afford the utilities. The Rich Church structures itself so that every three years it can explore the best options for ministry. Should it have a campaign or roll the debt into the budget? Has the church grown to the point where it can add another piece to the facility while reducing some debt? Have things gotten so bad that the church just needs a breather and should only pay interest for a year (which of course isn't possible if you are only paying interest presently)? The previously mentioned church had no net and now finds itself hanging by a thread.

"WE" WILL VS. "THEY" WILL

One of the huge mistakes that Poor Churches make is believing that those who will come into the church after it is constructed will be the ones who will pay off the balance owed. The misguided movie quote "Build it and they will come" is on the tombstone of many a church throughout the land. The Rich Church makes all of its plans with the understanding that those who are presently making the decision are the ones who will see it through. Granted, few should ever build with the belief that the new facility will not bring in new persons, but a church should not build a financial plan that mandates this happen for success.

When you as a church leader set up a plan that "they" will help make happen, you encourage less than a full effort from those who are present. Those present start to think that all they have to do is get the ball rolling, and others will keep it rolling. When others do not appear as hoped, then the ones who started things often resent having to maintain the push. This also can backfire with those who are looking at the church as a possible future home. If it comes across to them that perhaps your prime interest in them as a new family is their wallet potential and not their spiritual welfare, they will run to the hills and not to your altar. Either way, you lose.

When you ask your people to vote on a building project and go into debt, make sure that they understand that the entire burden of the plan rests with them and not with others.

BORROW 2X RAISED VS. BUILD IT…THEY WILL COME

The Rich Church determines the amount it should borrow based on only one number, and that is the amount that was actually raised in the initial capital campaign. It will not go by what the payments will be or what a lender says it will loan. The church will not go off its budget or some experience in raising money ten years before. It will run its capital campaign and make sure it does not borrow more than two times what was raised. Keeping debt at this level gives this church reasonable assurance that with one more campaign it will either eliminate its debt or so drastically reduce it that it can easily be rolled into the operating budget.

Keeping debt at this level also gives the church choices at the end of the three-year giving period of a campaign. If the church has grown substantially, it may well be possible to add some space while reducing the debt; or if things have turned negative for whatever reason, it can back off for a short period and pay interest only without suffering substantially. Either way, the discipline of never borrowing more than two times what the church raised should ensure that sound and solid ministry is never trumped by debt. Remember, the whole idea of debt is to enable ministry. You should go into debt for no other reason. As soon as debt becomes the focus, you have lost your way.

Look at the example of these two churches below:

RICH CHURCH	POOR CHURCH
Budget - $500,000	Budget - $500,000
Raise - $1,000,000	Raise - $1,000,000
Borrow 2X Raised ($2 million)	Borrow 3X Raised ($3 million)
Year Six Owe - $557,000	Year Six Owe - $1,816,000
Annual Payment - $66,000 (10 yr.)	Annual Payment - $218,000 (10 yr.)
% Budget - 10 percent	% Budget - 33 percent

The Rich Church adjusted its project so that it only had to borrow two times the budget, but the Poor Church felt that it could go ahead and do the whole thing, causing it to need to borrow three times the budget. That did not seem like too big a jump to the leaders at the time. After all, they had plenty from their one-million-dollar campaign to make the payments. Look at what happens to Poor Church, though, in year six. It has had two back-to-back capital campaigns. Both churches agreed that a third one would not be wise because of internal issues in the church, so they rolled the amount into their operating budget. In the Rich Church, the members had to adjust their giving by 10 percent to make that happen. Not easy, but doable. The Poor Church families had to adjust their giving by 33 percent. Crushing!

In most churches, salaries and benefits for staff amount to around 55 percent of the budget. The Rich Church can add 10 percent for debt service and will still have 35 percent left for programming and ministries. The Poor Church only has 12 percent remaining. In a number of denominations, the denomination request each year amounts to between 10 to 15 percent of a budget. What does the Poor Church have left? Nothing for ministry! When persons begin to see that ministry is not being done, they begin to leave a church, and even fewer dollars are available. New persons are not attracted to a church that is unable to be fully engaged with their family. No dollars gained. It becomes a downward spiral that was all caused because of a terrible decision regarding the amount of debt a church should take on. Before moving forward on any project or borrowing any amount of money, get a cash-flow analysis that will show you where you will be once your capital assets are no longer available. Then make a good decision.

QUESTIONS FOR YOUR CHURCH

1. Can you look back and see how a debt decision negatively affected your church?

2. What percent of your budget presently is debt? If debt was eliminated, what would your budget look like?

3. Do you have a solid and faithful plan to get rid of debt in your church?

4. Have you ever heard persons say, "Build it and they will come"? How did that work out?

CHAPTER FIVE

ASKING

RICH CHURCH	POOR CHURCH
Passion for Ministry	Fear of Rejection
Want to Succeed	Want to Please
See People Grow	See People Content
Treat Like Adults	Treat Like Children
Ask for All Things	Ask for All Things but Money

The Rich Church has learned that great gifts usually come from a great ask. The pastor and other leaders in the church are not at all afraid to share with someone what a gift would mean for the body of Christ and their hope that such a gift might come from that person. The Poor Church is also very aware of what great gifts could mean, but it lets its own comfortableness win out over service to the Kingdom. For the Kingdom's sake, we must get over it.

PASSION FOR MINISTRY VS. FEAR OF REJECTION

I visited with a man whose daughter had recently been accepted into a very good college. He was sharing with me what he had done.

"When that acceptance letter came in the mail, my daughter was overjoyed. It was her first choice, and she had worked very hard to make the competitive cut. We could not have been more proud of her and for her. The letter, however, noted that though she had been accepted she would not be awarded much of a scholarship. The amount owed for this school was far more than I could afford and beyond anything we felt comfortable letting her borrow. While my wife and daughter celebrated in the living room, I went to the den and pondered what I might do to make this happen."

"So," I said, "did you pick out a bank to rob or what?"

"No, I decided to take a trip up to that school and see if the president would see me."

"You did what?" I asked.

"I went to the school and got an appointment with the president. I told him that I knew he was not head of admissions, but I wanted him to hear me out regarding my daughter. I then proceeded to share with him what an incredible young woman she was and what an asset she would be to their campus. I went over her scores and stuff, but mostly I talked about things that would not be so obvious in a file. I talked pretty solid for about ten minutes, and then I simply shared with him that she could not come to the school without additional funds. I let him know how we had been responsible parents and she had been a very responsible student, but the amount of money necessary just would not work. Then I sat up straight and asked him for a full scholarship and I shut up."

"And?" I queried.

"Well, it did not happen right away. He asked a few questions. He told me that what I was doing was a bit unusual, but he respected my honesty and certainly could see the love I had for my little girl. He said he would look into things and I would hear back from the school. Two days later we got a call from admissions. Seventy percent scholarship!" he shouted.

It was a neat story, and I could not have been happier for him and for his family. I know what the president saw in this father, because I saw it even as he was sharing the story with me. His passion and love were so profound.

This is the key to asking for support from a donor. It does not matter if you are asking for support for the Boy Scouts, the local university, or the church. The key is the passion of the one who is asking. You don't have to be suave or a professional fundraiser. You just have to truly believe in your cause (ministry) and be unafraid to share that cause with someone else. Sometimes it is the passion that gets a commitment as much as it is the cause.

You may read this and think, "I don't have much passion for this place. It is hard to get excited about just paying these bills and patching up what is broken, but we have to get money from somewhere." If this is your response, forget it! Don't even think about asking. Go get a job at a place you do believe in and can be fully committed to.

Oftentimes I hear church leaders say that they are afraid to ask because they are afraid of rejection. What is rejection? It is simply saying that what you have now is what you still have. If you ask a girl on a date and she says no, you just have no date. You did not have one before you asked, either. If you ask a clerk to give you 10 percent off and the clerk says no, the price is still the same. You don't lose anything. You just failed to gain. When you ask someone for a gift, you will have one of two outcomes. One is that the status quo is maintained and you have no gift. The other is that you get the gift and can use it on behalf of what you are passionate about. Why be afraid of the status quo?

Preachers should be the last ones who fear rejection. They get rejected almost every Sunday after preaching the morning sermon. Yet most all of them get right back up and try again the next week.

WANT TO SUCCEED VS. WANT TO PLEASE

The Rich Church wants to succeed on behalf of the body of Christ. The church understands what additional funds can mean for ministry and in changing lives. It asks because it desperately wants to succeed. It knows, and Indiana University proved, that personally asking has been shown to increase giving by 42 percent over the amount of the gift when the giver was not asked.[1] If I ran a business and knew that dressing up in a chicken suit would increase my revenue, I would dress up in a chicken suit every day. Asking is easier.

The Poor Church simply wants to please. It knows that if it does not ask, very few if any persons will complain or demand to be asked. It runs absolutely no risk whatsoever. In taking as little risk as possible, it gets as small a return as possible. Nobody will grumble about the preacher spending too much time with money people, however. The church won't have nearly enough money to do effective ministry, but no one will blame the leader. In such a setting, pleasing takes precedence over the gospel.

SEE PEOPLE GROW VS. SEE PEOPLE CONTENT

When we challenge persons to give, show how they can give, and they actually give, they grow in their understanding and relationship with Christ. They come to realize that they cannot serve two masters, and in giving they find out that of the two, Christ is the only trustworthy master. Being taught how to give is as integral to the mature Christian life as learning how to read is to the adult life. The Rich Church knows this, and in its preaching and teaching makes sure that money and the need to give it are active and vital parts of the spiritual curriculum. Pastors and church leaders are not afraid to ask and challenge persons to give sacrificially just like a coach is not afraid to ask more of his or her players. Both want to see growth and maturity that will lead to a victorious life.

Successful coaches always say to their players that they can do more. They can run faster. They can lift more. They can hit harder. Successful pastors in successful churches always challenge their members to give more, serve more, study harder, and pray more diligently, because they know they can.

The Poor Church is primarily concerned with making sure people are content. It does not seem to take spiritual growth seriously. It may give growth lip service on Sunday morning, but in every other way it is just looking to find out what makes the congregation happy and do it. If expectations are too high or the request too straightforward, then people might feel uncomfortable. Giving money is like lifting weights or running miles. It does not sound like fun on the front end, before we see the effect, so many persons leave the cross-carrying to Jesus.

TREAT LIKE ADULTS VS. TREAT LIKE CHILDREN

The Rich Church treats its members like adults. They communicate in a mature way. While you may not talk about money matters too boldly with a child, you certainly can with an adult. You talk about the stock market and its ramifications. You talk about mortgage rates and savings and inflation. These are all adult topics when adults get together. When I am at nonprofit fundraisers, I am amazed at how easily persons talk with one another about what they are giving or hope to give and why. They even spend a good bit of time talking to other persons about why they hope these other persons will also give to this cause and occasionally how much they hope they will give.

I remember the first time I was at one of these fundraisers. A man I was casually chatting with said, "I think I will give this outfit one million dollars. What do you think?" I almost fell over but frantically tried to remain calm and look like I talked about a million dollars every day. "Are you sure you want to talk about that here with all these people?" I inquired quietly. He looked at me and said, "Clif, it is not life and death. It is only money." He wanted to have an adult conversation with another adult surrounded by adults. The Rich Church seems to understand this sort of thinking.

The Poor Church seems to treat most of its members like children. I have often heard a pastor—prior to preaching his prescribed one sermon a year on money and giving—offer a caveat such as, "Now I will be talking about money today. I just want to warn everyone beforehand." Such a comment is like saying the next movie is rated R, so you may want to take your children out of the room. That same pastor would not think twice about reading a verse of scripture about slaying thousands with a sheep's horn or ramming a stake into someone's brain. Oh, no, that is appropriate, but money is just something we shouldn't talk about. Give me a break!

ASK FOR ALL THINGS VS. ASK FOR ALL THINGS BUT MONEY

When I bring up to pastors and lay leaders that they should be willing to ask members to consider a gift, many will quickly respond that they are just not good at asking. "Really?" I say. They then tell me all the reasons that asking makes them uncomfortable and uneasy or why it is plainly inappropriate.

In response, I ask them how they go about getting Sunday school teachers. The answer is that they ask. I inquire how they go about getting persons to serve on their leadership board and councils. The answer is that they ask. I want to know how they go about getting new youth leaders, and they tell me they ask. I continue, how do you get someone to lead one of your summer mission trips? The answer is that they ask. I have found that one of the characteristics of the Poor Church is that it is willing to ask persons all the time to use their talents for the Lord's work, but never their treasure. Church leaders may go door to door to find three more choir members or to find people to work on a Habitat for Humanity house, but they will not even get out of the car to ask someone to part with their mammon for God.

The Rich Church does not see a difference. It asks for all that the Poor Church asks for and then adds money to the list. It knows that people need to give their treasure just like they need to give their talent. Jesus wants 100 percent of them, not 10 percent or 50 percent. They ask for it because they know the good that it will do for the church but, most especially, because of the good it will do for the church member.

QUESTIONS FOR YOUR CHURCH

1. Why do you suppose church leaders find it easier to ask personally for service than to ask personally for money? Is it related in any way to sin?

2. Do you ever see your church making decisions on the basis of what will keep people content rather than help them grow spiritually?

3. Do you see a passion for the gospel in your church? Where is it? Is this something that needs to be shared?

4. If you do not see passion in your church, why not? What would it take to get persons to want to share with others about what is happening and then ask for support so it can continue?

NOTE

1. *Advancing Philanthropy* (January 2010).

CHAPTER SIX

BEING
THANKFUL

RICH CHURCH	POOR CHURCH
Personal Notes	No Notes
Gatherings	Treat All the Same
Have a Choice	Obligated
Model Humility	Model Arrogance

As I write this, it is about two weeks before Christmas. Just about every charity in the nation is out searching for donors. Like many others, I get an end-of-the-year bonus at work, and I usually have some discretionary income that I want to give to deserving groups. I get phone calls, letters, pamphlets, cards, and newsletters from a whole host of nonprofits that want me to give them an end-of-the-year gift. In front of every storefront I hear and see the Salvation Army bell ringer with the red kettle. I also hear from the church. It, too, would like an end-of-the-year gift. I received a letter from the church. I now have to decide with which ones I will share a part of my wealth as we draw near Jesus' birthday. How do I discriminate regarding who gets what amount or any amount at all?

I see the letter from Campus Crusade. It is once again produced well, sharing with me information about specific college students that its ministry has affected. Each time I have sent in a contribution I have received a nice handwritten thank-you note. About once a year, I even get a personal visit from the campus minister to thank us.

I see the letter from my college. They have thousands of alumni, but I always get a nice handwritten note from the advancement office, thanking me personally for each gift. I have never given that much, but they always thank me anyway. I even received a checkbook holder one year that I still use.

In fact, as I look over the requests, I realize that most of the notes have been sent from persons who have in one way or another personally thanked me for my contributions. But not my church. It thanked me with a corporate thank-you that appears to be just like one that everyone else gets. It is the same letter that my friend across the street got, and he has not been in the church since last Christmas. It says, "We appreciate your faithfulness in the past year and hope you will consider an additional gift as we close out the year." His faithfulness amounted to $10 (he told me he gets mad because the church "wastes too much money"), and my faithfulness amounted to about 12 percent of our income.

The Rich Church understands that there is nothing inappropriate about thanking people for sharing their wealth, just as they thank those who share gifts of time or talent. We don't send everyone in the church a thank-you note when one member shares a gift of song. Instead, we send our note of gratitude directly to those who have sung in the choir or performed a solo. We don't send everyone a thank-you note when some church members go on a mission trip. Rather, we thank those who actually went. Why can't we specifically thank those who give sacrificially or significantly to the church? The Rich Church knows how to thank people for whatever they give. The church does it personally, and it means it. The Poor Church just takes people for granted, or at least gives that impression, which in the end is the same thing.

PERSONAL NOTES VS. NO NOTES

I have long been an advocate of personal notes from pastors to those who have done exemplary things in the church in giving or serving. I have been a major proponent of this simple strategy because receiving such notes never ceases to affect me. The other day I received a handwritten note card from a layperson who had attended one of my seminars. It shared how my message had changed her thinking and how grateful she was. Now, I got paid to give that talk. Several hundred persons were there, and many shook my hand and said thank you. Nothing had the heartfelt effect that this woman's six-sentence note did. It reminded me how important what I do can be and how I need to work even harder to improve. It made my day! Have you ever resented being thanked?

Pastors and lay leaders in the Rich Church understand that taking time to write personal thank-you notes is valuable time, and they block off minutes in each week to do exactly that. They make sure that statements to donors are individualized so that tithers are thanked by name and others are challenged to grow. They know it makes a real difference. The Poor Church just seems to do what is easy and quick. It is easier to write one note to everyone with the same challenge and a "faithful friend" heading. The church gives more thought to what will save fifteen minutes of time than to what would actually advance the Kingdom.

GATHERINGS VS. TREAT ALL THE SAME

Mike Slaughter serves a megachurch outside of Dayton, Ohio. Dayton is one of the most economically depressed areas in the country. This church, however, is one of the most mission-minded in the country, with a per capita giving ratio about double what other churches are getting. The church fits my definition of Rich Church.

Every year Mike holds two retreats. One retreat is for those who give at least $10,000 a year to the church, and the other is for those who give between $1,000 and $10,000. At those retreats he is able to do a number of things. One is to thank persons appropriately for what they are giving and to appropriately challenge them to grow from their present level. Thankfulness is a huge part of both meetings. Interspersed between these retreats are individual meetings that are held with various givers to personally thank them. Why does he do this? He does it because it is effective in securing funds so his church can continue to send over $2 million each year to missions in the Sudan. Thankfulness is given to specific persons in specific and individual ways because it helps ministry happen and lives change.

I examined a church not long ago and noticed that three donors supported over 40 percent of the church's budget. Three families out of nearly 150 were making ministry happen. I asked the pastor if he had ever made a personal visit to any of them to thank them directly for their support. He said no, because he did not want to appear to favor them over the other 147 families. Well, these three families held his entire church together and funded a huge part of every ministry that went on there. If any of the three made a different choice for one year as to what to do with their money, it would ruin this church. Tell me why a personal thank-you would not make sense for the Kingdom? This pastor would not have hesitated to thank someone who played the piano every Sunday so the church could have worship. I would guess that others in the church can also play piano but for some reason had chosen not to. Similarly, although many in the church have the ability to cut the grass, the pastor would not hesitate to thank the specific someone who mowed the lawn each week so it looks nice for Sunday services. No, he placed money in a gift category that was designated as not deserving of thanks, and someday when he really needs some financial help for that church, he may get an answer from these three of "no, thanks." Who does that scenario help? Treating everyone the same when it comes to gifts of money is a very unwise move if one really cares about growing the church.

HAVE A CHOICE VS. OBLIGATED

Earlier I described the choices I have in front of me this Christmas season. I have a lot of choices about where

I choose to give money. The Rich Church understands that persons have a choice, and it does not take their giving for granted. It does not act as if it is the only organization in town that is serving in ways that are pleasing to the Lord. When someone gives to the Rich Church, the church knows that it won out in an arena in which everyone does not win, and it is abundantly grateful.

The Poor Church maintains an attitude that when it comes to church giving, persons are obligated. Since they put their membership here, they have an obligation to give, and not just to give but give well. When they give, they are in essence just "doing their job" and do not deserve a special thank-you beyond that which would be given to someone who went to work and performed the assigned task as usual. Well, I had a very successful operation at the hospital. Am I obligated to give there? My daughter has enjoyed her time as a Girl Scout. Am I obligated to give there? My son had a positive experience with Campus Crusade while in college. Am I obligated to give there? My mother had Alzheimer's disease. Am I obligated to give to that foundation? My friend is active in a mission in India. Am I obligated to give there? None of the above organizations treat me as though I am obligated. They understand I do not have to choose them, and when I do choose them, they are grateful and say so.

MODEL HUMILITY VS. MODEL ARROGANCE

There is a humbleness of attitude in the Rich Church and a pervasive arrogance of attitude in the Poor Church. In the latter, the attitude seems to be, "You owe me, so pay up."

In the former, the attitude more often than not is, "You owe Christ for his sacrifice. I know there are a lot of places and groups doing the work of our Lord, and we are ever humbled that you have chosen to express your thanks by giving to us."

QUESTIONS FOR YOUR CHURCH

1. Specifically, how is thanks expressed in your church? Is it personal or corporate?

2. For laypersons: have you ever received a personal thank-you note from a pastor? How did it feel?

3. What would be the reaction if the pastor intentionally sought to meet with and thank the most significant donors to your church?

4. Do you feel that your church presents an image of humility to the donor, or do people hear more often that they are obligated?

5. Should the church outrank other Christian organizations (rescue missions, food banks, hospices, Habitat for Humanity, etc.) when it comes to giving? Does this have anything to do with performance or just the fact that the name of the organization includes the word *church*?

CHAPTER SEVEN

EXPECTING

RICH CHURCH	POOR CHURCH
High Expectation	Low Expectation
Classes Mandated	Classes Are Nice
Disciple	Member
Tithe as Benchmark	Proportional Giving
Sign Covenants	Receive Certificates
Getting Started	Finished

HIGH EXPECTATION VS. LOW EXPECTATION

"But the gate that leads to life is narrow and the road difficult, so few people find it.... Not everybody who says to me, 'Lord, Lord,' will get into the kingdom of heaven. Only those who do the will of my Father who is in heaven will enter" (Matt 7:14, 21).

The scripture above is from the end of the Sermon on the Mount. Jesus was just beginning his ministry, and his disciples had not yet been fully trained or deployed. Jesus had just finished going over for them what the Christian life was like when it came to behavior and lifestyle. It was radical. It was certainly high expectation. Jesus pulled no punches here or later in his many discourses to those who wanted to be disciples.

Later, as he deploys the disciples, he commands them to go and do as he has done and make more disciples (Matt. 28:19). I see nothing in the scripture that states that the expectations are to be lower or minimized in any way. The standards for discipleship were, are, and always should be the highest possible. The job is just too important to expect less.

The Rich Church is a high-expectation church. In fact, if I were forced to identify one singular characteristic that differentiates the Rich Church from the Poor Church, it is expectations. The expectations in the Rich Church, much like Jesus' expectations with his disciples on the mount, are expressed from the beginning, lest anyone get confused about expected standards for character and behavior.

Quite frequently I see in the Rich Church more persons in worship than exist on the membership rolls. The simple reason is that membership means something in these churches, and many persons are just not ready to make that bold a commitment. In the Poor Church, you will see 20 to 40 percent of the membership present on any given Sunday. It is just not a big deal and never has been.

Statewide newspaper *The Arkansas Democrat-Gazette* ran an article on churches that were growing and those that were not. It noted that the fastest growing denomination in America was the Church of Jesus Christ of Latter-day Saints, or the Mormons.

In reading through the article, I ran across several comments from the church leaders. One noted that when they construct a new church building, it is always paid for before the first worship service. He said, "Mormons don't pass an offering plate on Sundays. Members are expected to tithe, meaning they give 10 percent of their income to the church. We live the law of tithing and we live it strictly. Money for construction, for humanitarian aid, for education all comes from tithing. That is the Lord's money."

The leader went on to say, "Membership comes at a cost. Members are expected to tithe. They are expected to attend worship services and to volunteer in service.... The church expects things from their members. When you are a member, you are a member 24/7, even when you are sleeping."[1]

I was struck by how many times the word *expect* was used in the article. Church leadership did not shy away from stating what the expectations of membership were in a very clear fashion. They did not say *proportional giving.* They said *tithing.* They did not say *serve.* They said *two years in missionary service.* They did not just say *attend.* They said *attend every Sunday.*

This church is growing at a rapid pace, while almost all mainstream Christian denominations are in a free-fall decline and are looking for any warm body they can find to occupy a spot in a pew. The difference is clearly one of expectations. Most mainline Protestant churches and my Catholic friends tell me that they suffer from the same disease of extremely low expectations with little or no standards taught prior to membership. Even after membership, expectations are shared with a sense of apology. Accountability is nonexistent. What these churches have found is that when it comes to giving, service, and attendance, their people have lived up to the low expectations that have been set. This has translated into giving of less than 2 percent of income, membership roll attendance of 35 percent, and missions at the lowest level in the nearly fifty years of counting missions spending.[2]

In February of 1991, the world witnessed the ground invasion of Iraq by the United States and a coalition of over thirty nations. Nearly one million troops were assembled in Saudi Arabia—500,000 of whom came from the United States—to evict Saddam Hussein and his army from Kuwait. Such numbers were needed because Saddam had an army of over one million soldiers with up-to-date equipment and munitions. The thought of most experts was that it would be an extremely tough fight to get through the Iraqi infantry, artillery, and armor units.

When the ground offensive started, led by the First Armored Division of the United States Army, the first Iraqi troops they encountered quickly came up out of their trenches and out of their bunkers and surrendered without firing a shot. At the mere sound of an approaching American helicopter or tank, they waved white flags, threw up their hands, and gave up. The allied forces were initially and considerably slowed down, not by the fighting, but by having to deal with prisoners of war. Later on some fierce battles took place, but aided in large part by this first wave of surrenders, the American and allied forces marched into Kuwait in four days and saw an army of one million fold its tent and go home. They had been defeated!

What had happened? Quite simply, though about one million soldiers existed on both sides, the Iraqi first-line soldiers did not want to fight. They had been recruited or drafted, outfitted with a uniform and a rifle and sent to the front line. They were not trained, however, to fight. They wanted nothing to do with the conflict. Many did not even believe in the cause. The Iraqi officials had just taken any able-bodied man they could find off the street and placed him in the army so they could strut around saying, "Look how big and bad we are." In truth, of their one-million-man army, only about 250,000 really had an expectancy to fight.

I fear that what we have done in the church is to recruit the Iraqi army as Christ's army. We have laid out low expectations, if any at all. We have not fully trained our troops before bringing them in as "full members." We have checked to see if they were upright and breathing and then placed them on the roll as quickly as possible. They received an ID card and a name tag, but we never fully expressed a set of expectations.

When the pastor preaches that it is time to rise up and engage a world full of unbelievers, march boldly against social ills in society, give powerfully to the starving around the world, and spread the gospel to our neighborhoods, most of the congregation just throw their hands up and surrender. So in the face of fewer and fewer persons claiming Christ as Savior, more and more going hungry, flourishing discrimination, abounding addictions, and rumors of war, the church has not led. It has thrown up its hands and waved the white flag.

CLASSES MANDATED VS. CLASSES ARE NICE

The Rich Church will almost always mandate classes for anyone seeking to join the church. Expectations regarding membership in the Christian faith community are fully outlined for attendees. These classes range from four to twelve sessions and take place over two to twelve weeks. They are designed not to orient persons to the local church, such as location of rooms, names and positions of staff, type of business structure, and so on, but primarily to orient persons to the nature of discipleship. Much emphasis is placed on financial stewardship, worship attendance, Bible study, and volunteering outside the walls of the church.

The Poor Church maintains an attitude that attending an orientation class is nice but certainly not required. To require it would mean that some persons would not want to join because of the inconvenience. This would then mean that at the end of the year there would be fewer people on the roll. Some would also question the appropriateness of such classes because of a misguided theology of works righteousness. "Aren't we supposed to be open to all comers?" they may ask. How we have abused grace to the detriment of the church.

Yes, the church as the body of Christ is to be open and loving to all persons and to invite them into our fellowship. However, the church also owes its invitees an explanation of the expectations associated with accepting an invitation. Expectations have nothing to do with whether they receive love and grace. Rather, expectations are a sign of a person's willingness to commit in a mature manner. It is abundantly clear in reading the Gospels that Jesus reached out to all but did not make them all disciples. He maintained a very high standard of discipleship. Ask Nicodemus or the Rich Young Ruler. Jesus wanted to establish a church that would be his body on this earth, a church whose purpose is to bring all persons back into relationship with the Father. This requires a lot, like carrying a cross or going against mother and father. If persons truly accept and live up to these standards, Jesus said he will change the world and establish his kingdom on this earth. In other words, church membership is a big deal.

DISCIPLE VS. MEMBER

The Rich Church is always focused on making disciples. It wants persons to be true followers of Jesus Christ. It talks about discipleship rather than membership. It understands that membership implies that you are owed certain privileges by the organization. Discipleship, however, underscores that you have no privileges but instead have taken on responsibilities of service to others. In the Rich Church, it is clear that the customer is outside the walls of the church. In the Poor Church, there is a heavy concentration on serving one another within the walls.

TITHE AS BENCHMARK VS. PROPORTIONAL GIVING

Let us be clear: a tithe means a tenth. To give a tithe is to give one-tenth of what God has given back to God as an offering of love and thanks. I consistently hear churches refer to anything given by persons into the offering plate as a tithe. Let's see what happens when we straighten out our language.

In the Rich Church, you hear sermons and lessons on tithing as the benchmark expectation in the Christian faith. In nearly every Christian denomination in existence it is seen as the biblical standard. It is not seen as a legal number, which once achieved gets one to heaven faster than any other action. It is seen as the benchmark to be taught and hopefully exceeded by Christians as a spiritual discipline and symbol of who our God is and who our God is not. In the Rich Church, this is clearly laid out in membership classes, from the pulpit and from articles written regarding financial stewardship. The church is extremely clear and precise: tithe is one-tenth. This is the standard, and this is the expectation at the Rich Church.

The Poor Church uses the word *tithe* with great hesitation. It is viewed as unachievable by most and thus inappropriate to mention with any degree of expectation or even seriousness. It alters the language to say, "We expect persons to give proportionally." Now, what does that mean? What is a proportion? Is not one penny of my income a proportion of my income? Is that what you are happy with? Is that what you are saying is good for my spiritual welfare? It does feel a lot better than actually giving me a standard that I can measure against and about which to feel good or bad.

SIGN COVENANTS VS. RECEIVE CERTIFICATES

I witnessed a final membership class in a Rich Church for which I consulted. Persons present had spent some time being taught the eight expected actions of the church. Before leaving, each person set up an appointment with his or her assigned pastor to write a covenant statement regarding all eight of these expectancies. The pastor then helped each person ascertain if she or he was prepared for membership, and set up periodic meetings during her or his first year to use covenant statements to assess growth in discipleship. It was powerful, and it was biblical. It was taking seriously that "marrying into the body of Christ" is a major responsibility that is to be taken earnestly with full integrity.

In the Poor Church, you do not see persons signing covenants of standards or benchmarks designed to encourage growth. Poor Churches instead repeat a couple of sentences that can be interpreted in a multitude of ways with no serious accountability. At the end of this two-minute process in front of the church, new members of a Poor Church receive a certificate that is suitable for framing but gets tossed into a drawer and quickly forgotten.

GETTING STARTED VS. FINISHED

Persons joining the Rich Church are constantly reminded that they are just getting started in the Christian life. They no more fully understand the total demands of discipleship than newlyweds understand marriage. The covenants and pledges are all designed to help them move out from wherever they are to grow closer to Jesus. They will no more meet the standard perfectly right off than a new husband would. But the standard should be known and fully committed to right from the start. Progress is then made each day to grow closer and closer.

In the Poor Church, the attitude is that once a person joins, he or she is finished with his or her obligations. New members take a vow, shake a hand, and are sent out into the wilderness of a congregation or community to fend for themselves. A true indicator of this is to see how many churches have evangelism committees but no assimilation committees: Get 'em to the altar and wish 'em well. It is better to help them finish.

QUESTIONS FOR YOUR CHURCH

1. Does your church express high expectations or low expectations? How?

2. Do you have required classes prior to joining?

3. How many persons in your congregation know the difference between tithes and offerings or that *tithe* means 10 percent?

4. Have you ever heard the phrase *proportional giving* used in your church?

5. What would happen if your new member applicants were asked to sign covenants on discipleship before joining?

NOTES

1. Christie Storm, "More Mormons," *Arkansas Democrat-Gazette*, (December 12, 2009): Religion, 16.

2. *The State of Church Giving through 2009* (Champaign, IL: Empty Tomb, Inc., 2011).

CHAPTER EIGHT

KNOWLEDGE OR IGNORANCE

RICH CHURCH	POOR CHURCH
Know Donors	Guess on Donors
Stewards Lead	Reputation Leads
Pastor Leads from Facts	Pastor Leads from Hope
Aware of Sin	Blind to Sin

I sat with two pastors reviewing some statistics I had requested about their churches. Both were having significant trouble getting their bills paid, and both were extremely frustrated that their whole ministerial focus was being spent trying to balance the budget. Each one had filled in two pages of data related to their church.

I looked up at one of the pastors and said, "Are you aware that you have one donor who is contributing 42 percent of your total income?" He answered, "I knew that we had one big donor, but I did not know exactly what the percentage was." "Do you know who he is?" I asked. He said, "Not exactly, but I think I can figure it out."

I looked at the other pastor and said, "You had one

family contribute $500,000 in your last capital campaign. Do you know who this is?" He replied, "This happened the year before I came. I am not sure who that was."

Are these the responses of leaders who want to serve the Kingdom as a first priority? Ignorance is not a good thing for churches.

The first pastor did not recognize that the future of his church resided in the wallet of one donor. He had spent very little, if any, time working on a strategy to thank the donor, discuss a planned gift with the donor, or develop a plan to broaden support for the congregation to which he was responsible. He intentionally ignored the financial data because he felt that it somehow was the proper position for a pastor to take. He refused to know anything about individual donors by either looking or even talking with the treasurer. I was in possession of the data because the pastor had asked the treasurer to send it to me directly, so his eyes would not be tempted to peek. This pastor was not a foolish man. He was, in fact, very thoughtful in the way in which he did his ministry. He was doing what someone had told him was wise many years ago and had never thought what damage such a position was potentially causing. Ignorance of the source of support for his church was no virtue.

The second pastor did not know because the church hid the data from him. The church treasurer was absolutely sure that his arms would be cut off and eyes plucked out if he shared one piece of financial data with the pastor. This had been the tradition of this church from its inception, and rarely had a pastor ever challenged it. The current treasurer and members of the finance committee faithfully enforced it. How ridiculous! This church had a family generously donate one-half million dollars, making a new building for their church a reality, and the pastor had no idea who they were. He could not thank them if he ran into them. He could sit across from them in their own home at a dinner party and be absolutely unable to say thank you or to inquire as to what their motivation was or how they determine what or to whom they give. He could only talk about football or church landscaping. The president of a college would have called this family personally and asked them to his home after they made such a gift to the college, the executive director of the Boy Scouts would have visited the family to see if they would mind a new camp being named for them, and the chairman of the board of the local hospital would have invited them in for a luncheon in their honor and put a framed picture of them on the wall in the new neonatal unit. But the senior pastor of their church just remained ignorant. This antiquated policy and misguided thinking does not advance the mission of the church.

KNOW DONORS VS. GUESS ON DONORS

The Rich Church believes that it is always better to know than not to know. When a pastor chooses not to know something that can be known, that pastor places himself or herself a disadvantage.

Would the world have been better off if General Dwight D. Eisenhower had said that there were certain things about the enemy that he just did not need to know before D-day?

Would the president of a corporation help his company in any way if he chose to remain ignorant about some of the facts on the ledger sheet? Ask the Enron executives if their defense of ignorance about what their company was doing held up in court. The best leaders lead from a position of knowledge about their company. They want all the data available to assist them in making decisions that shape the future course of their organization. Ignorance is just never a good policy. The leaders of the Rich Church know this. They are never afraid to lead.

In my consulting experience, it seems that sometimes leaders of Poor Churches prefer to lead by guessing rather than by possessing actual knowledge. They don't know who their donors are but seem to rely on intuition. Amazingly, they claim to understand the importance of knowing donors' identities, but believe they can correctly guess who those donors are.

Imagine that the commanding general of the army appeared before Congress and was asked by what information he had made a major decision on sending American forces into harm's way, and he replied, "Oh, I just guessed. I have been a general for a long time, and I know what to do. I don't need any data."

Similarly, what would you think of a company president who says that she does not need to know her largest customer but instead claims that she has a pretty good idea who it is and just deploys her salespeople accordingly? She is pretty sure she is right. I would not buy stock in that company. Yet this is exactly the position we want our pastor to take on when guiding the body of Christ. Guessing does not serve the Kingdom.

STEWARDS LEAD VS. REPUTATION LEADS

Not long ago a church paid me a considerable fee to do a thorough study of why their finances were perpetually bad. The pastor was very concerned, and many lay leaders seemed to carry the same concern. They wanted me to fix the problem. I studied the church's financial picture for several days and in doing so realized that little I could say or do would make any difference. This church had a wall of defense that I was not going to be able to conquer, and neither could the present pastor or perhaps any pastor. Its first impenetrable wall prevented anyone except the treasurer/financial secretary from knowing what anyone gave. This secretary kept all these things and pondered them in her heart. But this was not the biggest problem. It had just helped create the biggest problem.

The biggest problem, and the second impenetrable wall, was the finance committee, who set the rules on financial information sharing. Only three or four members of that fourteen-member committee gave more than $2,000 a year to the church, or were among the top one hundred donors to the church. The pastor, who sat on the committee, was one of those top givers. The chairperson of the committee was not.

I knew that my recommendations would call for this church to select leaders in a very different way and to hold them accountable. My recommendations would call for radical changes in the way stewardship was taught, preached, and practiced.

These recommendations would have to be approved by this same committee before any other official body could rule on them, and I knew that the committee would never approve of them. Sure enough, they did not get passed on. The pastor called and told me that the committee had simply voted to table any discussion until a later time. He was sure the recommendations would never come up again. This church's stewardship problem was that the persons in charge of finances were not willing to lead or challenge others to go where they themselves did not want to go. Case closed!

The Rich Church has systems in place to ensure that leaders are indeed leading. Persons who are financial leaders lead in finances and persons who are song leaders lead in singing and persons who are mission leaders lead in missions. Usually it is the pastors of these churches who are tasked with approving the nominations list so that no one is elected or chosen who has not met the standard of leadership, which is not to put on a good show, but actually to be a disciple of Jesus. The church does not just want those who say, "Lord, Lord," but those who are actually doing the work of the heavenly Father.

The Poor Church puts persons in leadership who have a reputation for leadership either in the church or in the community. They have this reputation because they always seemed to be on a committee or positioning themselves to be a part of making a decision: "We always take Joe's advice when it comes to the budget"; "Bill has been the president of the bank for twenty years, and he knows what we can raise and spend." This sort of process leads to crises such as occurred in the aforementioned church, in which the committee may be full of finance professionals but is empty of finance disciples. The chairperson of that finance committee had been in the position for eight years and was not about to give it up. However, he did not deserve to keep it.

PASTOR LEADS FROM FACTS VS. PASTOR LEADS FROM HOPE

As mentioned earlier, if you are a pastor and you do not lead from facts, then you are simply leading from hope. All pastors "hope" they have donors in the right position. All pastors "hope" their people are exemplifying the Christian life and following Christian disciplines. In the Rich Church, pastors take whatever is available to give them real facts about giving, worship attendance, volunteer service, and spiritual growth classes, and then help persons get into positions in which they lead others.

In the Poor Church, pastors refuse to look at much beyond whether a person fits a specific social profile. If they find the right balance of members for their committee or team, they roll with the flow, believing they are serving their Lord. They are not!

AWARE OF SIN VS. BLIND TO SIN

Would you allow a known thief to serve on your finance committee? This is not an ex-thief or a reformed thief, but an active thief who for whatever reason has not been arrested. I am assuming you would say no. If this person's sin caused him to make decisions that served his need to steal more than it served the need of the church to make disciples, it would potentially harm the church. My guess is that if a pastor nominated someone like this to the committee, some members of the congregation would go to him and encourage reconsideration due to the current practices of this person. It would help to know whether a member has the church's best interest at heart or if sin is controlling his or her actions.

As disciples and church leaders, we rightfully keep watch over the actions of people in our communities. For example, no right-minded leader would allow a child molester to work in the children's department. If such a person were even considered, many would protest and demand reconsideration to protect the children and potentially the whole church. Everyone would be very afraid that a person like this might not be able to control his or her propensity to sin, to the detriment of others.

A pastor needs to know about the history of persons asked to serve in any capacity, whether in the children's ministry or in the finance ministry. Is it good leadership to allow persons who have made false idols for themselves to serve on a finance committee? Is it responsible to allow a person to serve on a finance committee, to help make decisions that affect the distribution of God's money, if she or he has obviously chosen to serve mammon rather than God? Does the Bible not explicitly give us guidance on this? Yet, because of the ignorance of God's chosen servants, in the majority of our churches we have persons who worship the money they carry and the homes they have built and the toys they play with far more than they worship God. These same persons would in a heartbeat rather make a business deal on the Sabbath than be in the house of God. Many would choose a ball game, horse race, or trip to a casino over worship on Sunday. They spend large sums on automobiles, boats, and planes, yet give a pittance to the church or to God's work. These persons get chosen to be our finance leaders because they seemingly know a lot about money. The problem is that although they may be financially savvy, they obviously know very little about Jesus. These blatant sinners of money run many Poor Churches.

The Rich Church is well aware that the chief sin is the worship of money and material things. It works diligently to help persons addicted to this sin go through recovery and come to accept Jesus as their Lord, rather than things. Church leaders do not put these material addicts in charge of the recovery center (church) until they are fully recovered, because they know that once these people are in power, they will perpetuate the addiction. Rich Church leaders are not blind to financial sin, and readily encourage persons to deal effectively with it.

The Poor Church seems blind to this sin. It wants to talk about lots of other sins, but seldom does it want to deal with the sin that has most of their leaders in its grasp. After all, pointing out sin to the sinner is not a pleasant process or experience, but it is the first step in helping people overcome.

The bottom line is that in any area of life—including finance—the more we know about the sins of our congregants, the better hope we have for putting together a leadership team that will lead people to follow Jesus, and not worship idols.

QUESTIONS FOR YOUR CHURCH

1. Why do you think that people would object to the leader of the church being fully aware of the revenue stream that supports the ministry of the church?

2. Is there a process whereby leaders in your church are screened to help ensure that they are qualified spiritually to lead in the areas they are being asked to lead in?

3. Do you see any Kingdom reason why it would be better for the pastor to lead from hope than from facts?

4. What is the chief sin in your congregation?

CHAPTER NINE

STEWARDSHIP WITHOUT APOLOGY

RICH CHURCH	POOR CHURCH
Stewardship Is Life	Stewardship Is Forbidden
Frequent in Worship	Stewardship Is Once a Year
Offering Is a High Moment	Offering Is Time-out
Pastors Model	Pastors Hide

STEWARDSHIP IS LIFE VS. STEWARDSHIP IS FORBIDDEN

When I was in the army, we ran every morning. We got up, brushed our teeth, put on our running shoes, and ran. If we were in a specific training unit, we ran with that unit. If we were off on our own doing a specific task, we ran alone. Either way, we started our day running. It really was not something we thought about very much. We understood the importance of doing our job, and we just did it. Running was very much a part of who we were and what we did. If someone were to suggest having a meeting first thing in the morning instead of running, everyone would wonder why. Our DNA was to run.

The Rich Church is sort of like that with financial stewardship. It is just a part of the culture and DNA. The church talks frequently about it. It is a part of every worship experience. It is discussed in most classes. It flows throughout the church. People don't make a big deal out of it. It just is.

The Poor Church puts financial stewardship in a category all by itself, like an unwanted church program. It is like the puberty talk. You go off in a room where no one else can hear you and you talk in hushed tones and do it as quickly as possible. It comes across as forbidden fruit that should not be on public display. If the Poor Church is ever to become a Rich Church, this attitude must be overcome. It will take time. If you are an army leader and you have an army that does not run and your goal is to instill running, it does not happen just by declaring, beginning tomorrow we will now run every day. The church is the same way. Most of our churches have kept financial stewardship in the back room and have only brought it out once a year, for a short while. A long-term plan must be put in place through which in time stewardship feels right at home in the living room of our lives.

FREQUENT IN WORSHIP VS. STEWARDSHIP IS ONCE A YEAR

I sat in a worship service that was at first a wonderful, worshipful experience. The youth choir sang, and their fifty voices rang out. The church was full, and it seemed that all present sang the initial hymn. Then about twenty minutes into the service, the pastor introduced the finance chairperson. This man came to the pulpit and said that although Christmas was a wonderful time of the year, it was also the time of the year the church had to get its financial house in order. He referred to Christmas as "Black Friday" and said the church's entire financial year would be made on what the congregation gave over the coming few weeks. We were then informed that an extra $400,000 was needed, which would require a record offering. He described the percentage of money that December had to produce and how far behind the church was with the denominational askings. By then I was lost in bewilderment. I wanted worship. I wanted to get into the experience of my Savior being born and ponder the mystery of this special season. Instead, I got retail sales and a dose of financial shortfall. I just wanted out of there. Worship started up again and went for another thirty minutes, but I was stuck on the need for $400,000. This is a Poor Church. It will most certainly be begging again next year.

The Rich Church would not have done this. It would never substitute a worship experience with a finance committee meeting for persons who had come for worship. What it would have done is have one of the fifty youth come up and give a testimony on how the church has influenced his or her life, or show a video of the church in ministry throughout the year. Then leaders would have shared how an end-of-the-year gift can make a significant difference, and then passed the plate. This would have enhanced worship and enhanced a person's willingness to give. The Poor Church chose a strategy that discourages people from giving.

The other sad part of this experience is that the church

potentially lost several families who were visiting for the first time. Christmas is the prime time for "new customers." Every church-growth study I have ever seen emphasizes how Christmas is the time when more unchurched persons come to church than any other time of the year. When you force these visitors into a finance meeting with a report on a drastic shortfall, it does not make them want to return. When they don't return, they don't wind up as donors. Worse than that, if this is the first worship experience they have had in years, it may have just become the last worship experience they will ever have, and you have seriously failed the Kingdom in trying to win this person to the cause of Christ.

The Rich Church communicates this sort of financial information to its membership, but does it in private e-mail or letters that are read and understood by the membership. It uses a targeted communication campaign in which those who are tithing and giving in exemplary fashion are thanked, and others are asked to give in appropriate ways to which they might respond. It is not shared with the unchurched, and it certainly is not forced into a worship experience.

OFFERING IS A HIGH MOMENT VS. OFFERING IS TIME-OUT

The offering is probably the least prepared part of worship. We rehearse songs for hours. We meticulously plan sermons. We give much thought and contemplation to prayers. We pick hymns with great deliberation. Then there is the offering: "We will just stick it here."

In church after church after church, I get the feeling that

the offering is not taken very seriously. It is usually a "time-out" from worship. You can assume that after about twenty to thirty minutes you will get a chance to check your cell phone for messages or write a note or whisper to your spouse because it will be the offering time and that is not really worship. This is a Poor Church.

The Rich Church makes sure this time is well integrated into the worship experience. Members share testimonies or stories right before asking persons to give so that ministry gets emphasized rather than budgets. As the plates are passed, you hear special music that fits in with the worship themes of the day.

PASTORS MODEL VS. PASTORS HIDE

Prior to doing a seminar for several hundred church leaders, a pastor who planned to attend called me to talk about plans for his church. We went over many of the customary questions about project rationale, cost, and timing. We covered the size of his church and what they might reasonably expect. It was a good conversation with a man who had been a judicatory leader but who was now serving one of this denomination's large churches. He asked if I would mind meeting with him and his committee following the seminar, and we set it up.

As soon as the teaching day was over, this pastor was waiting for me. He quickly asked if he could talk with me prior to our meeting with his committee. We went off to the side. He said, "I heard you say loud and clear that you have very high expectations of the pastor as the leader in financial stewardship. I will not argue that point. You also talked about how the pastor needed to share what he or she was giving in any campaign so as to model the Christian response to the congregation." I nodded that he was hearing me correctly.

His next words caught me off guard. "My committee members are here today to hire your firm to run our campaign. They are prepared to act, and frankly after the presentation are more ready than ever. However, I need to know, if we hire you, will you expose me? I am not a tither, and I am not even close. I tell my people that I do not want to see the giving records and neither should anyone else except our treasurer, so none of them know. I doubt I will be able to give very much to the campaign. Can you keep my secret and still work with us?"

This was a stunning confession from a pastor who was in a high position of leadership in his denomination. He had obviously been able to keep this secret throughout his career, and he wanted to make sure that his secret would not be exposed during the campaign experience. I told him that we had no desire to "out" anybody on anything but that he needed to do some serious soul-searching in regard to this part of his life. The campaign was run. The pastor was not exposed and, of course, did not testify. He claimed righteousness in not wanting to even see a pledge card. The campaign was a modest success due to some outstanding lay leadership. This pastor is now assigned to yet another church, and as far as I know he is following the same stewardship path he has always been on.

In the Rich Church, the pastor is always the model for commitment. Be it a commitment of time for a mission trip or a commitment of tithe, the pastor is up front in saying, "Follow me." These pastors will share either in a yearly letter or from their pulpit exactly what they are giving from what they are making. They are very transparent in giving leadership in this arena. Like Paul, they are not afraid to say, "Imitate me." These pastors share how they arrive at their tithe decision, be it net or gross (and I think it should be gross). They share how they make decisions on what to spend for Christmas and vacations. They share how they go about determining what to give to other worthy causes and why they do so. They talk about how they determine what "offerings" to make over and above their tithe discipline. They share, not so they can brag, but so they can lead. Pastors are not perfect people but are children of God just like their congregants. However, they are the ones set aside by their ordination to lead persons in growing into the likeness of Christ. They are on the journey just like everyone else. They are just at the front of the line. Pastors should be able to say, "If you will follow my example, it will not make you perfect or ensure your ticket to heaven, but it will help you grow into the likeness of Christ along with me." The Rich Church pastor is not afraid of modeling Christian behavior when it comes to giving.

In the Poor Church, we quite often see a pastor who is not and could not model Christian giving behavior. That pastor wants to hide. The excuses are numerous and run from "My spouse will not let me" to "My finances are all messed up with debt" to "I have two kids in college and I failed to save much for that" to "I give more than 10 percent of my time and count that as my tithe." None of those excuses are biblical reasons for not sharing our first fruits with the Lord. They show low spiritual esteem and will invariably lead to a church with a perennial financial crisis. In twenty years of working with hundreds of congregations, I have never seen a Rich Church with a pastor who did not lead in financial stewardship. Never!

However, in about 80 percent of the Poor Churches I have worked with, I see a pastor who is trying to hide and is incapable of modeling Christian behavior when it comes to giving. As I frequently say, "The sheep ain't going where the shepherd ain't leading."

QUESTIONS FOR YOUR CHURCH

1. How often do you hear life-changing stories during your worship services?

2. Is financial stewardship something that is a known part of the DNA of your church, or would most members think it was a once-a-year thing?

3. What is the offering experience like in your church?

4. Do you feel that the pastor, as spiritual leader, should model financial stewardship for the congregation, or should he or she just keep all financial giving to himself or herself?

5. How is the pastor expected to be different from others in the congregation?

CHAPTER TEN

TRANSFORMATION

*Do not be conformed to this world, but be transformed
by the renewing of your minds, so that you may discern what
is the will of God—what is good and acceptable and perfect.*
—*Romans 12:2 (NRSV)*

*"Go therefore and make disciples of all nations, baptiz-
ing them in the name of the Father and of the Son and of the
Holy Spirit, and teaching them to obey everything that I have
commanded you."*
—*Matthew 28:19 (NRSV)*

"You must be born from above."
—*John 3:7 (NRSV)*

RICH CHURCH	POOR CHURCH
Changing Lives	Paying the Bills
Need of the World	Guilt
Giving Changes Us and Them	Giving Balances the Budget

CHANGING LIVES VS. PAYING THE BILLS

The word in the Scriptures seems abundantly clear that the aim of the faith is to change us from following sin to following Jesus. One does not become a Christian by conforming to the world but by being transformed through the love and grace of Christ to a new life. We are to be changed or born from above so that we, as disciples of Christ, might then change the world, helping usher in the kingdom of God. This is why we exist, and the business that every church is to be in. We are in the changing, transforming business, and the more we share with persons that we are successful in that business, the more they will shop in our store.

In the Rich Church, you hear a lot of discussion of how transformation is taking place. Persons constantly testify about how they were once addicted to drugs or alcohol or sex or gambling and how the church led them to understand the transforming nature of Christ and how life is now new. Stories appear in newsletters and on websites that tell how a person used to put work before family and how their children suffered and a marriage crumbled. Now through the work of the church and the power of the Holy Spirit they are together again and focused on each other as the greatest gift God could give them. People who are in worship see videos of persons doing mission work in a Third-World country and how a little girl with a serious illness was cured and how her family is now happy. They see members of their church laboring in the hot sun in Mexico to build a house for a family of eight who has had nothing more than cardboard walls and a tin roof for the last ten years and then witness the joy on the family's face as they move into their new home.

In the Rich Church, the total focus is on transformation and how change is making a difference in the world. Persons are encouraged to give to help continue this transformation. People crave the opportunity to make a difference in the world, and the message of this church is that its people can be the vehicle that helps bring about change.

When people give to see change and transformation and then hear how it was done, they are immediately compelled to want to give again and to give more to make an even bigger difference. It is a beautiful cycle.

The Poor Church puts 99 percent of the emphasis on the obligation of its members to pay the bills. On Sunday morning, letters are sent or messages are delivered that address the shortfall and how a budget was set or a project was once approved that must be fulfilled. The Poor Church's leaders talk about denominational askings and how they are fairly set for all churches and how the church is obligated to pay those bills. This is simply another mind-set of the donor that the church is seeking to appeal to. The problem with it is that it is becoming less and less effective.

The World War II generation is one that is inclined to fulfill obligations. Persons who grew up in this generation are motivated by this argument. They don't want the denomination's leaders to feel badly about them. They feel identity and pride in their church of the last fifty years and will do all that they can to uphold the good image of the church to the denomination. If there is an outstanding debt, this generation wants desperately to pay it off and relieve the church of this obligation. The Poor Church structures almost all of its financial communication so that it appeals to these persons who are seventy years old and older.

The obvious problem with this is that each year there are fewer and fewer of the over-seventy crowd, and they are not being replaced by twenty-somethings. If they are replaced by the twenty-somethings, the church quickly finds that these families do not give anywhere close to the level of the over-seventy group. We keep communicating with these new families just like we did with the ones we just buried, yet wonder why the money only trickles in.

The issue is the way we are trying to motivate. Generation X and the Millennial generation could care less about denominational obligations, unless you can convince them that the payments are really changing lives. They feel no obligation. They could care less about past decisions that incurred debt. They want to know if the decisions triggered any transformation. Did it affect lives? They don't care that you have bills you can't pay. They want to know what those bills bought that changed children or helped the youth mature. Congress can't pay its bills either, and these generations are not clamoring to pay more taxes just to help them out.

One of the easiest ways to identify a Poor Church and a Rich Church is just to look at the website or read the newsletter. You have a winner if either one is full of stories or examples of transformation. You have a loser if the accent is more on the organization.

NEED OF THE WORLD VS. GUILT

Rich Churches constantly talk about how the church is there to address the needs of the world. It exists to feed the hungry and clothe the naked and bring sight to the blind and care for the sick and visit those in prison. The church sees itself as a prescription for a sick world and each member of the church is called upon to be a healer and helper. Ministry from Sunday morning to Wednesday evening to Saturday morning is done to respond to needs outside the walls of the church. This is why we give. The customer is outside. Giving becomes a way truly to make a difference, and the donor feels good in doing so, which then causes the donor to want to give more. The pastor and leaders give out lots of applause to such generous and faithful congregants.

Poor Churches communicate a message of guilt. Shame is often heaped on the congregants for not living up to their vows: they promised to serve and to give, and a significant percentage have not given or served, and only a small percentage comes on Sunday. Shame on you, church! Persons should not be beaten and prodded to give. They should be helped to understand the difference that their giving makes.

It is the difference between positive versus negative motivation. If you believe that beating your children works better than showing them the positives that come from proper behavior, then go ahead and try this with the congregation as well. If you think that yelling at your spouse and reminding him or her of your vows works, then go ahead and try this with the congregation. If you think that constantly fussing at your employees and reminding them of the obligations of their paycheck is more effective than rewarding achievements with such things as recognition, a small bonus, and an extended lunch break, then try this with your congregation.

Remember, people really do want to make a difference. If they are not giving to the church, it is probably because they see something else making a bigger difference. Help them see how they are making the world a better place, and they will pull the wagon of Christ all day long. Whip them too much or shame them with guilt and obligation, and they will lie right down in the road and refuse to go any further.

GIVING CHANGES US AND THEM VS. GIVING BALANCES THE BUDGET

As I look back on parts of my sixty-year-old life, or at least the ones that I can recall, I am struck by what a poor steward I have been for most of it. I have been a tither for all of my adult life. In fact, I have generally found that between 12 and 20 percent of my gross income has been given away each year; yet I confess to God and to you, the reader, that I have not been a good steward. I say that because I see how much of what God has given me has been wasted. If I had trusted him more, how might he have used me? What might he have done with me, had I been a better steward?

I do not regret the purchase of any of the three homes I have owned in three different cities in which we have lived. Those homes provided good shelter for raising our children, getting them an education, and staying healthy. I do not regret what I have been able to put into my pension account and additional saving funds. These expenditures will help my wife and me fully care for ourselves without being a burden on our children. I don't regret what I put into my business, because it has gone on to serve thousands of churches that have in many instances done profound work for the Kingdom.

I regret what I spent on cars. From the time I got married and bought a small orange Mazda, I have purchased, usually with borrowed funds, about thirty-five vehicles. They have ranged from a three-quarter-ton Ford pickup truck to a four-wheel drive Jeep to several minivans and SUVs. They have been used and new and salvaged. We've had at least two in the garage for over thirty-five years. On all but the last few I lost considerable money in interest and depreciation. Looking back I see that at least 50 percent of these vehicles served no more useful purpose than the vehicle I already had. I did not need a Jeep just to go hunting three or four times a year. I sure did not need that Dodge Charger to get me to work, but it looked so cool. I bought that big Ford truck so I could haul firewood, which I did about twice a year. Every car I traded ran just about as well as the one I bought to replace it. I wasted tens of thousands of dollars on cars. That is poor stewardship!

All during this time I was tithing, and I am so thankful for it. I do not look back and regret one dime that I gave away to the churches I have been in. I shudder to think how wasteful I would have been if I had not had this discipline in my life. I can only imagine how deep in debt I would be today if I had succumbed to the notion that more and more "stuff" would be exactly what my life needed. Tithing the first fruits of whatever I earned at least gave me a good platform to establish priorities in my life. Now my confession is that I did not build upon it perfectly, and I still have work to do, but it would have been a lot worse if tithing were not in place. Today, finally, both cars in my garage are over five years old, and I paid cash for them after satisfying my tithe commitment and other priorities first.

Tithing has changed my life and the lives of my children. All of them have adopted tithing as a foundation in their lives, and it has helped them prioritize expenditures much more appropriately as they have entered adulthood and have started families. It has reminded us all of what is most important, even as we are constantly tempted by a consumer society.

Tithing has helped us feel a partnership with God and learn to trust him over the bulge in our wallet. Nothing in life is more important than knowing in whom we trust and establishing our lives accordingly. Tithing has helped do that for me and for my children. It truly has been a blessing. It is truly amazing. In my forty years in ministry, I don't think I have met a tither who was not happy. Most tithers I know are content and fulfilled. They seem to know who they are and whose they are. I can't say the same for Sunday school teachers, pastors, missionaries, music directors, or others with exemplary traits nearly to the degree as I can of those who practice tithing. I can't tell you I fully understand why, but that is certainly what my experience has been.

The Rich Church is well aware that giving is a spiritual discipline and a spiritual decision. It has very little to do with money, but it has everything to do with our devotion to Christ as Lord of our life. It is easy to fool ourselves into believing that we have a good relationship with our Savior until we are put to the test of giving and then are forced to see what we truly trust. The Rich Church constantly addresses giving from a spiritual platform, calling persons to examine their heart over their head or wallet. The Rich Church pushes people to ask spiritual questions regarding their giving rather than financial questions. It actually talks about what our new cars, cruises, clothes, and toys have to do with being a disciple.

The Poor Church concentrates on balancing the budget and staying in the black. They do not measure spiritual health but financial health. If the budget balances, then the Poor Church believes it has been successful. I vividly remember witnessing a finance committee chairperson stand up in a worship service a few years ago to announce during Lent that the committee had slashed the budget to the degree that for the first time in eighteen months the budget was balanced. The membership in attendance applauded loudly. What were they applauding? Being in the black? When I later asked the pastor for a copy of the new budget, I saw that the children's, youth, and young adult ministries had been zeroed out. One staff person had been removed, and the denominational asking had been cut by 75 percent. It balanced the budget, with members now asked to give only about 60 percent of what is normally given in a healthy church, but it gutted ministry. This got a round of applause. This is a Poor Church in spite of its having a balanced budget. We are in business not to balance budgets but to change lives, do ministry, and make disciples. I wonder, if someone had come up that Sunday and been baptized, would it have gotten applause the way the balanced budget did?

QUESTIONS FOR YOUR CHURCH

1. In your church, do you hear more transformation or obligation?

2. Have you ever witnessed guilt being used as a motivator in your church?

3. Do you ever subtly imply that if the church budget got balanced then the church had had a "good year"?

4. How has giving changed you or anyone you know?

5. When is the last time you heard a good sermon on the spiritual value and discipline of tithing?

CHAPTER ELEVEN

BECOMING A RICH CHURCH

If you are a "rich" church pastor serving a "poor" church, or if you are a church with potential but a poor past, how do you go about becoming a Rich Church?

As a new pastor or lay leader, you have opportunities that others do not have. The long-tenured pastor has accepted certain practices and procedures and has preached a certain message for some time. To suddenly be faced with a new word from an "old wineskin" can be very confusing to a congregation. Being new brings a certain expectation that things will change and an openness from a congregation to at least consider change, if for no other reason than to accommodate a new pastor.

It has been twenty years since I was last given a congregation to shepherd, and many of the practices that I have observed that make a Rich Church were not on my radar back then. With that disclaimer, I can say that I have not forgotten what was helpful to me and what mistakes I made. Taking my experience and adding in twenty years as a consultant, observing some of the best and worst in leaders, consider this plan for becoming a Rich Church:

WEEKS 1–6: DATA REVIEW AND ANALYSIS

First, work to understand all the facts and history that have brought the church to where it is. Look into worship facts, giving facts, building facts, and any and all moments that seemed to bring significant transition. I would chart these on a time line to see what relation any had to another.

After obtaining the data, set up gatherings for staff and lay leaders to listen to the data and to share their understanding of it and what congregational feelings were at the time. It is very important to put facts and feelings together. Seek hard to cast no judgment upon the facts or on the comments made. Understand the past to help cast a different future, but don't judge a past you weren't a part of.

WEEKS 1–12: FOUNDATIONAL PREACHING

While you gather data, your preaching and outward projection need to be on the foundations of your faith. Your preaching needs to help persons know you and know who you know. You have just come to lead people in a faith journey, and they have a right to know what makes the leader tick. For that reason, your preaching needs to be on the fundamentals. I remember one church member saying to me during the first month of a new assignment, "Preacher, we know your credentials and schooling. Now we want to know if you are a Christian."

A bishop said to me once, "I am going to ordain you, but you will have to be reordained again each time you get to a new church." He did not mean that I would physically have other persons lay hands on me but that I would have to earn their trust. It does not come just because some church hierarchical leader said so.

Any hope you have of moving your church from Poor Church to Rich Church over the course of your first year will be dependent on your gaining the trust and confidence of those you hope to lead.

WEEK 13: FORTY HOURS OF PRAYER

After about three months, retreat alone for forty hours of prayer. Do this during the week, preferably on a Monday to Wednesday. You might take a couple of books with you that will help you focus your prayer and study time. Your primary mission in prayer and devotion is to hear from God what the mission is to be for your church and your ministry in that church. Is there a land out there that is better than Egypt? As you come to some understanding of what your calling is, pray over how to raise the level of discipleship beyond where you are. The people in your church have been where they are for a long time. It requires change and commitment to pack up and leave the familiar for a wilderness of the unknown. Can you see the cloud that goes before you?

As I look back on my own attempts to lead faithfully, my greatest failure was to rely too much on my own wisdom and not nearly enough on God. I did not retreat by myself enough or open myself fully to the leading of the Holy Spirit. I knew that we should not stay in Egypt and that there was a better place, but I did not know how best to do it and I did not let the Lord draw the road map. When I said, "Let's go," it far too often sounded like Clif was leading instead of following the Lord's leading. My people knew the difference.

As I have worked with and studied the work of those whom I consider "Rich Church" pastors who are leading their churches to be incredible witnesses to God's love and might, I see how they have used their times of prayer and retreat so effectively. Do not overlook this vital piece of the puzzle.

WEEK 14: LEADER RETREAT

One week after getting back from your retreat, while things are still fresh, have an overnight retreat with ten to twelve of your key leaders to share with them what you have learned from your time of prayer and devotion as it relates to God's calling for the congregation.

Prior to going, review your thoughts and findings with a single key leader and get feedback from that trusted person. This will help you discern how best to share with the entire group and also will give you another voice of support—an Aaron—as you seek to bring the leaders along.

Your goal here is to share with them what God has revealed to you regarding mission, expectations, and path. All is certainly open for discussion and for debate as you wrestle with discernment, but remember, if you truly feel God is calling you to go somewhere and he is prepared to lead you, it is not negotiable. Be bold in your convictions. In fact, if you are not prepared to be bold, then you need to go back on your retreat and stay until you are. Your people want to go where God wants them to be, and you are their leader!

At the conclusion of this overnight retreat strive for a solid consensus on mission, expectations, and path. Let each leader present speak to whether he or she personally feels called to help lead in this journey. Let them know that over the next few weeks you will be asking persons to step up and help lead the congregation, and that you really want to hear from each one of them on whether they feel called to this important task or not.

WEEKS 15–24: CHOOSING LEADERS

Moses chose seventy; but then, he had hundreds of thousands to lead. Unless your church has hundreds of thousands, you don't need seventy on your Exodus Expedition Team. You will need no more than twelve and perhaps as few as six. They must all be leaders in every discernible way: worship, serving, giving, and witnessing. These people must know Jesus! They must not have any other agenda than faithfulness to the leadership of God in moving the church in this new direction. Select a couple of excellent books on what the church can be and what discipleship looks like, and study these together (look at authors such as Bill Easum, Lovett Weems, Leonard Sweet, Adam Hamilton, or Mike Slaughter for ideas).

This is a good time to deliver a series of sermons on the new vision and what the promised land looks like. Avoid criticizing the past or even the present. It does not matter. All that matters is where God wants you to go.

Also during this time it is wise to hold a couple of open forums or town hall meetings to listen to congregation members express their opinions regarding the direction of the church. Introduce the Journey Leaders. Establish a rule that nothing is off limits for discerning what God may be calling the church to, and no one can be against any idea that is expressed. Your job and the job of the leaders is to listen. You will be coming back later to talk.

WEEKS 25–40: JOURNEY STARTS—CHANGES BEGIN

During this time is when you start to leave Egypt. Not everyone will leave at once, and it is wise to phase changes in. Changes should begin to take place around worship, finances, evangelism, mission, education, staff, and so on. All these changes are necessitated by the call to leave where you are for where God wants you to be. Each change must be clearly worked through with your Journey Leaders and taken to whatever appropriate ruling bodies exist. Each change has to relate back to the call. Tread lightly through this time, and, working with your leaders, carefully craft the timing of changes specifically as they relate to staff. Remember, keep your eye on the destination and understand that the wilderness has hills and valleys. There is nothing fun about this phase. But if you were diligent in your work in the previous twenty-four weeks, things will go much easier. This will be where your leaders have a chance to really shine. They need to walk alongside you when you begin taking those steps toward change.

WEEKS 41–52: OUT OF EGYPT—JOURNEY ONGOING

You will not have arrived at the end of your first year, but hopefully, all major shifts have been made, and the church is focused on the Promised Land. You will not have crossed over, but you will no longer be waiting on persons to leave. Some will have chosen not to follow, and that is fine. They may choose to stay in Egypt or may prefer a destination different from the rest. Again, that is fine. No judgment should be cast. Your job is to lead those willing to follow in the direction you feel God is calling you, not to make sure 100 percent of the people are in agreement. Remember, Jesus asked many to follow him, but only a rare few accepted. He still stayed focused on seeking first the Kingdom.

WEEK 53 AND BEYOND

Now consider major initiatives required by the transition. Capital and building campaigns may be forthcoming. Obviously these should have already been on the minds of the Journey Leaders, but nothing concrete should have moved forward until now. It is at this stage that you open these possibilities to the congregation, hold forum meetings, and start down the approval process toward implementation.

WEEK 65

It will have been one year since you retreated for prayer and devotion to help you focus on where God was calling your church. It would be an excellent idea to repeat that process again so that in the quiet of your study time and prayer time you can check to be sure that you have not misunderstood anything amidst all the noise of the journey.

Keep your Journey Team intact for at least another year. Meet with the team once every other month or so to reflect on changes, to review data, and to be certain all are still focused on the mission of being God's people where you are planted.

AFTERWORD

As I conclude this writing, it is ten days before Christmas. In the outer office I hear the sounds of "O Little Town of Bethlehem." Tonight I will once again gather with my family around the Advent candles to read the Scriptures, hear devotion, and pray as we focus our lives on this gift that soon will be celebrated. Unto us a child is born...a savior Christ the Lord.

This Savior who came in a manger on Christmas morning has never left me. He was with me before I entered the earth and will be with me on the day I leave this earth. He was with me in the midst of combat, witnessing death and tragedy. He was with me as my children were born, witnessing great joy. He has accompanied me down paths of righteousness and has been in the valley of the shadow of death. He was there each day that I stood in a pulpit and tried to share his Word. He was there as I stood over graves and tried to give understanding and hope. He was there as I buried my mother and was there a few years later as I performed the wedding of my father to a new love. He was there in Haiti as I tried to explain to a young, crying mother why I just could not accept her baby girl and take her back to America for a better life. He was there in Mexico when we handed the keys to a new home over to a family who had never had one. He was there last night as my eyes closed and was there again this morning when they opened.

I don't know what I would have done or what I could have become if this wonderful Christ child had not come into my life. It is the greatest gift anyone could ever receive, and he never stops giving. Every gift I have given and every gift I will ever give is just one small way of saying thank you, God, for caring enough to come to me and never leave.

Giving to the church matters a lot. This child who came grew up and gave his life for me and for you. This is a big deal. A very big deal! My prayer is that he is in every word in this book and that his Holy Spirit will guide and direct you as you read it and use it to help more persons understand this gift that has been given to them, as well.

CPSIA information can be obtained at www.ICGtesting.com
Printed in the USA
LVOW04s1208270815

451652LV00001B/1/P